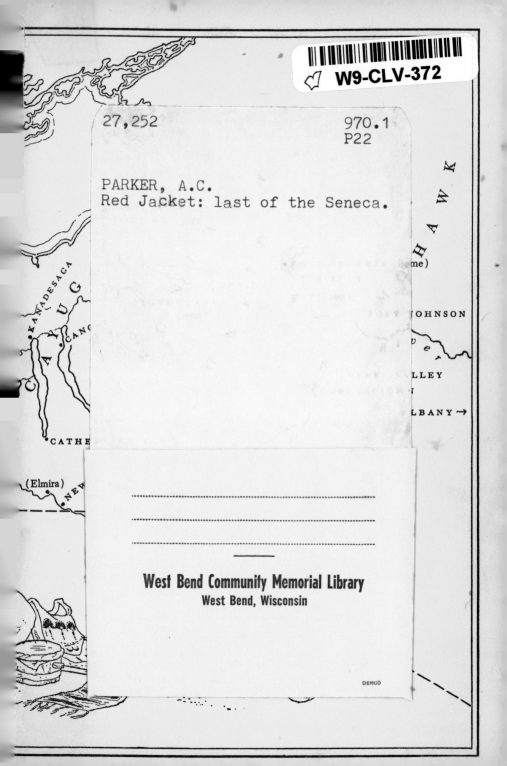

Red Jacket

LAST OF THE SENECA

ARTHUR C. PARKER

Drawings by Jack Moment

McGraw-Hill Book Company, Inc.

NEW YORK   TORONTO   LONDON

To Martha Anne Parker
who roamed the Red Jacket Trail
and drank from the bubbling spring at Canoga

PREFACE

Red Jacket, the noted Seneca chief, was known far and wide because of his persuasiveness and skill as an orator. It was often asked how a man who was uneducated in the ordinary sense—he had never studied books—could think so clearly and deeply. Red Jacket's answer was that he had listened to men of wisdom and had heard the voices of nature.

In his early years Red Jacket learned from his mother that truth is a powerful weapon. The use of it, however, got him into trouble many times, because people do not like to hear the truth if it is unpleasant. Yet he would state his arguments with logic and force that made his opponents sorry that they had tackled him. Because of his conscientious efforts for the welfare of his people, he became one of the most famous leaders of the League of the Iroquois, the group of Indian nations to which the Seneca belonged.

Red Jacket was born in 1750. On his tenth birthday, in the customary tribal ceremony, he was given the name Otetiani, meaning "Always Ready." When he reached manhood, he was awarded the title Sagoyewatha, which is translated "He keeps them awake." The name Red Jacket was bestowed upon him, not by his own people, but by British soldiers who gave him a red coat. Thereafter he always wore such a garment when he appeared in public.

Red Jacket was a young man at the time of the American Revolution. He did not believe in war and had spoken earnestly against it. Furthermore, to fight the settlers would, he said, lead to the ruin of the Indians. Nevertheless, he took part in the struggle against the colonists because his people had reached the decision to aid the British.

During the War of 1812 many Iroquois, angered at the encroachment upon their lands by American settlers, wanted to join the British of Canada in a war of revenge upon the American states. The fury of this temptation affected the tribes along the Great Lakes. Again Red Jacket sensed the folly of conflict and warned that his people would be the losers. He made a clear argument against aiding the British and urged his people to support the Americans if war must come. They declared war upon Great Britain and defended the Niagara frontier. Red Jacket became a captain in the United States Army.

Before the Revolution the Seneca owned what is now western New York State. Red Jacket was determined that his people should have fair treatment at the hands of the whites who rushed in after the war as settlers or who came to make land treaties with the Indians. He resisted every move of the white man to expand his ownership of land held by the Seneca. If an acre were to be given up, Red Jacket believed that an honest payment should be made. He was, therefore, embittered after the Revolution when the Seneca were deceived into "selling" to American land companies all their land from the Finger Lakes to the Pennsylvania line. For this loss he blamed his own people and his brother chiefs, whose childish faith—that they "should never know want again" because of the pittance received for the land—had been their undoing.

In addition to his efforts to protect his people against the folly of war and the greed of white land speculators, Red Jacket gained prominence for his support of another cause. He possessed a steadfast belief in the customs and attitudes that had been important parts of the Seneca way of life long before the appearance of white settlers in America. He believed that the Indian pattern of life was best fitted to assure the survival of his people and that they would be ruined by the adoption of the white man's way.

He did not object to the white man's civilization for white men, although to him it seemed both inconsistent and hypocritical. But he constantly urged his people to cling to their own customs, purifying them if need be. It is with respect to this losing struggle that Red Jacket was truly "the last of the Seneca."

War, land, and Indian culture were the subjects of many dramatic councils in which Red Jacket won the respect of Indian and white alike. He became known as the greatest orator in America, even though he spoke only in his native tongue and his speeches had to be interpreted by white men who had lived with the Indians. Many prominent citizens of Buffalo, New York City, Philadelphia, and Boston loved him and entertained him in their homes.

For his own people he was too far ahead, and they repudiated him twice. To the cunning land-grabber he was a tormenting obstruction, to the clergy he was a hopeless pagan, and to the non-Christian Indians he was the white man's friend who had married a Christian wife. He was a paradox to many, but on occasion his opponents defended him against others. The missionaries stood for him against the land buyers who gained their ends by dishonesty, and the trader argued for him against the forces of temperance. He was ever in the midst of a dispute. When he spoke for himself, he silenced his detractors.

The people of New York State have honored Red Jacket in many ways, and two statues stand to his memory: one at his birthplace and one in Forest Lawn Cemetery in Buffalo. A large medal that George Washington gave him as a testimony of friendship may be seen at the Buffalo Historical Society.

Time has not dimmed the memory of Red Jacket, and poems about him are still recited in schools. His boyhood homeland in the Finger Lakes area and the land where he lived in his old age honor him by using his name for many good things, such as schools, lodges, clubs, and Boy Scout councils. He will long be remembered as a stirring force in the pioneer history of our country.

ARTHUR C. PARKER

CONTENTS

[1] *ALWAYS READY*
AWAKENS TO A PROBLEM

When the bark buildings of a town began to crumble about their ears, the Seneca Indians in the days before the American Revolution had a ready remedy. They simply built a new town several miles away and carried all their belongings to the fragrant new houses. There was no mess to clean up; a new settlement was easily put in order. Birds build new homes every year, but the Indians thought that ten or twelve years between towns was better.

Often towns had walls of tall pickets all around them, causing the white men to call them "castles." One such

1

castle west of Seneca Lake was becoming old and difficult to repair. The wise men, agreeing with the women's council, thought that a new settlement should be sought elsewhere, but there was one other reason why a clean and convenient town should be established. The old place was too remote from the east-west trade route over which traders carried their heavy loads of beads, iron goods, and bolts of woolen cloth. Traders wanted to enter a settlement without straying from the central trail that crossed the territory now known as New York State. And the Seneca wished to encourage the visits of the traders.

It was quite clear that the Seneca people of the ancient town should build anew, for the old houses rattled and crumbled when laughing French traders tried out their new axes on the corner posts. When Old King, chief of the town and ruler of the eastern Seneca people, decided that the time had come to build a new town, his orders were obeyed.

Thus, though Red Jacket, the hero of this story, had not yet been born and named Otetiani, the new settlement was ready to receive him and to provide the training that finally would make him a leader of all the Indians of the eastern part of North America.

The new town was called Kanadesaga, and in it lived some of the noted Keepers of the Faith, masters of the religious rites of the nation and recorders of ancient wisdom. Often they had proclaimed that the grandsires of the race of True Men, as the Iroquois called themselves, had discovered the only true way to live. The Seneca people nodded their heads in agreement, for they, too, belonged to the Iroquois League. It was generally agreed, therefore, that it was the strict duty of every child to follow the paths of his ancestors and to resist any change that might destroy ancient customs. This was the deep belief of the Seneca when Otetiani opened his eyes to the world more than two hundred years ago.

All about the child were customs and legends that immediately began to mold his life. Myths and legends were told at night around the campfires or within the bark houses of the towns.

One legend that later Indians liked to hear was about Otetiani's parents. We shall call him by his Indian name, for he was not yet known as Red Jacket. The story relates that Thadahwahnyeh, a tall young man from Skoiyase, the nearby Cayuga village, had often been a visitor at Kanadesaga. Indeed, the young Cayuga tribesman had helped lug the heavy poles for framing the lodges and had peeled many sheets of elm bark to cover the houses when the town was being built.

The story tells us that Thadahwahnyeh had been attracted by a bright-eyed maiden whom he called Blue Flower. He had been observed gazing at her with a fond look in his eyes as she dipped water from Castle Brook. His mother, or maybe it was his grandmother, had encouraged him to look for a wife, but he had seen no maiden of the Cayuga nation whom he thought half so wonderful as Blue Flower of the Wolf clan. Warily he waited for a sign of her approval, hoping she had noticed him.

This stoical young man may not have been of the nation of Old King, ruler of the town, but he was of his clan, the Turtle, and that helped. Thus, when one of the watchful matrons poked him in the ribs and said, "I'll get her mother to ask your mother," he felt greatly encouraged. The custom in those days was for the bride to be or her mother to make the proposal to the mother of the prospective groom.

And so it was that the girl's mother made a basket of boiled bread and carried it to the lodge of the young man's mother. The custom was to call, leave the bread at the door, discuss the suitability of the marriage, and then see if the bread were taken in and eaten. Once there was a nibble, the pact was sealed and "Yes" had been said.

Blue Flower's bride's bread was received and eaten with relish amid kindly words of approval and laughter over the shyness of the pair. The marriage proposal was announced in the council house, and somewhat later the couple was invited to the chief matron's lodge. There, seated opposite one another, they were lectured on the hazards and duties of marriage. Each was told the duties of a mate and warned that neither one was perfect. Each, therefore, must be tolerant and kind, must overlook faults, and must never argue over problems in the heat of anger. When the two agreed that they would live together in harmony, Blue Flower's tied braids were thrown over the groom's head and around his neck. After that Blue Flower must wear her hair in a single braid looped up in a knot to show that she was no longer single.

Following this ceremony and a feast, the couple were invited by the clan matrons of Across-the-lake village to make their home there, at least during the honeymoon year. The couple agreed, possibly because Across-the-lake lay in Cayuga territory and in the pleasant valley of Canoga Creek. The site chosen for their abode was Thadahwah-nyeh's own hunting lodge on the loamy bluffs between the creek and Cayuga Lake, a scenic spot shaded by elms and one giant sycamore tree.

Here near Cayuga Lake in the land of the Cayuga was a region of many wonders. To the south were high-splashing waterfalls, numerous trout streams, and a marvelous spring that had a stimulating taste. Blue Flower was entranced by this spring. It was deep and wide, and its waters gushed forth at all seasons. Tiny bubbles burst to the surface as if there were some living force beneath that drove the waters upward through pockets of air. There were legends about this pool and a strong belief in its magical qualities.

Blue Flower often peered into the depths of the bubbling water and as often wondered about its copious flow, noticing that it burst forth a full-born rivulet that ran northward until it turned east to meet the waters of Cayuga Lake. As she dipped from the brook and tasted the clear, cold liquid, she compared it with the murky water that flowed past her parents' hunting lodge on Crooked Lake, a full day's walk away. She spoke to her husband about the difference, and he replied, "It's magic water because the Great Spirit has spoken to it."

As a hunter and warrior, Thadahwahnyeh often had been urged to bring his beaver pelts to the trading post at Kanadesaga, and it was while he was there that he had been asked by the British to help fight the French who came down from Montreal. English traders and military men who frequently visited Old King had no love for the genial Frenchmen who came with baubles and brandy and struggled for trade with the Indians in the name of their king.

Many of the French traders lingered long among the

Seneca and Cayuga, spreading knowledge of the white man's world, his religion, his ideas, and his might. Thadahwahnyeh had also observed that white men who had fled the restraints of civilization and who dwelt among the Indians became more and more like Indians and less like white men. The number of these runaways became greater as time went on. The Indians, while they welcomed the refugees, were curious about them. Indeed, it was from such men that they learned the white man's history, his desire to possess the new continent, and the glory of the Old World across the sea. Some Frenchmen, however, were openly hostile to the civilization of their own race. There can be little doubt that their contempt for European ways greatly impressed the Indians. Thadahwahnyeh must often have heard white men spin their fantastic yarns in the lodges of the sachems, and he saw many a Frenchman adopted by the clans. On such an occasion the adopted brother learned that a clan was a group of families that had the same totem; that is, the same bird or animal symbol believed to have been used by a maternal ancestor. The Cayuga people had eight or nine such clans, and the Seneca had eight. Members of a clan felt that they were related to each other by strong ties. Some clans had sachems, or civil chiefs, and forty-nine of these sachems formed the governing council of the Iroquois confederacy of the Five Nations. With the adoption of the Tuscarora nation in 1722, Indians of the Five Nations became known as the Six Nations.

Though a young man, Thadahwahnyeh had traveled many trails and had dressed the pelts of hundreds of beaver, marten, and mink. The pelts were good sources of income.

However, he found the rates low at times and prices for clothing, guns, and ammunition high. The white traders were clever in making bargains. It cost a good many fine beaverskins to buy cloth, linen, silver rings, and brooches for the women and hatchets, powder, and kettles for use during his long sojourns in the beaver lands. Two yards of calico cloth, for instance, cost one beaverskin.

But now there was a happier time, and he determined to spend it with his young wife at the hunting lodge on the bluff overlooking the valley of Canoga Creek. The couple lived alone beneath a grove of elms, but an older woman often looked in to see that all was serene. This welcome visitor was Mrs. Fish Carrier, who knew that very soon a child would come to bring happiness to the young people.

The older woman knew that Across-the-lake village was a good place in which to be born, and as she gazed across the little valley, it seemed to be enveloped in a mystic aura. The old people, she recalled, used to say that a man would live happily in the world hereafter if he tasted Canoga water and carried some of it into his grave. The Great Spirit created the water, the old people said. He made it with a splash of a tear because brothers would not be peaceful. That was something for the young couple to think about.

Indeed, there was much to think about and to question in the ominous year of 1750. For instance, why did the French and English fight about beaver? Why did they encourage Indians to die if necessary in the attempt to obtain the skins of these wonderful animals? What good was trade if it didn't make everybody happy? What good was it if it made men hate each other? Trade seemed to make human

friends, and then the three were given space in one of the long houses of the Wolf clan. The Cayuga father was welcome, too, for men were needed as hunters. Chief Old King was a member of Turtle clan, and this made Blue Flower's husband a clan brother, quite a fortunate thing. As a result this child of Canoga for many years after was called by the English "the young prince of the Turtle clan." British traders thought that the boy was the possible successor of Old King. Some time later the son of Blue Flower was dubbed "prince of the Wolf clan." This, too, was incorrect because the Seneca did not have princes and no son of a sachem was allowed to succeed his father.

Kanadesaga, or Seneca Castle, was a teeming settlement that, until the American Revolution, overlooked Seneca Lake from the hills of its western bank. It was surrounded by cornfields and orchards, and its gardens were lush with many of the vegetables that the white man had, as well as Indian plants. In the center of the town was the council house where ceremonies were held. It was in this long house that the boy was given his first welcome to the nation, and there ten years later he received the name Otetiani, meaning "Always Ready."

In the latter ceremony he was presented with a string of precious wampum beads which was ever to recall his name and which attested the rites that had made it legal. He could never forget the great feather dance which he joined after his name had been proclaimed to the four winds. In all their feathered finery the dancers had circled the benches in the center of the lodge and had gesticulated in a wild fashion. Singers had thumped their turtle-shell rattles painted with a red cross and circle on the under side, and there had been cheers at the end of each part of the ceremony. "Who-eey!" they shouted in a high voice, dragging out the word.

Then followed a long thanksgiving ceremony in which the chanters thanked the Creator for everything He had made; for waters under the earth, grass and shrubs, trees, hills, mountains, moon, sun, stars, and the celestial world beyond the sight of mankind. Between sections of this thanksgiving hymn everybody danced in a graceful way. Through this rite Otetiani learned that, if one is to be remembered by the good forces of the universe, one must be grateful. That is why everybody said, *"Nyahweh"* when a good thing happened. It meant, "Thank you."

It was a grateful Otetiani who walked out of the council with his mother—a man of ten years with a real name and a wampum string to prove it. That name would be his until he could be given a grownup's title. However, if he did something wrong, his name could be taken from him and he would be a nameless outcast. A Seneca boy must guard the honor of his name! He vowed he would do that, and so long as he lived, whatever happened, he would be Always Ready.

He was not much older when he began to take long walks around Seneca Lake, visiting the deep ravines and numerous waterfalls. He saw Watkins Glen, Buttermilk Falls, and the high, plunging Taughannock, a beautiful cascade that is more than forty feet higher than Niagara Falls. His favorite haunt as he grew older, however, was Montour Falls near the town where Catherine, a woman chief, ruled her community with a lashing tongue and a commanding eye. Some people called her Queen Catherine and named her village Catherine's Town. It has been said that this famous woman often talked to the youth of Canoga and put strange ideas in his head, but it is quite evident that he also had ideas of his own.

Some of these ideas were new ways of looking at old things; some were old ways of looking at new things. To him nature supplied the key to all thinking, and he was fond of comparing everything he saw or heard with the facts of the natural world about him. Life was like water; it flowed on like a river and then entered a great sea and mingled in a vast pool of life. Old age was like a tree whose branches had been broken by storms and whose trunk had become weather-beaten and decayed. Good words were like flowers that bloomed and bore seed that lived on after the flowers had withered. Perhaps many of these sayings were echoes of words he heard in the council lodge at Kanadesaga, for the language he spoke was capable of many beautiful allusions. In time these niceties of speech were to give him great popularity in clan and tribal meetings.

Always Ready lived with his mother most of the time because his father had gone on a journey of war and had never returned. It is said that he had gone with Sir William Johnson, the British commander, when Fort Niagara was attacked and the gallant French were defeated in 1759. It was believed that he had been killed there.

Otetiani never wanted to forget that his father was a Cayuga. When he was taunted with the cry, "Your father is a Cayuga!", instead of fighting, he would glory in the fact and count it a high honor. Was not Logan, the orator and border chief, a Cayuga? He was a noted man. What if the

Cayuga had hunted in far places and had come back with captives with whom they had intermarried? The Seneca had done the same and counted it no defect. Was not a Cayuga as good as a Frenchman or an English captive, and was he not as able in council and hunting as the white refugees? Why talk about blood mixture? It is what a man is that counts.

Again and again this questioning youth sat silently in the councils of his elders, drinking in every word and storing wisdom in his mind. He found the old way good; the men it had produced were the heroes of his people. The troubles he saw about him, he was told, were caused in part by the goods and the temptations that the white man brought to the Indians and by the inability of the Indians to resist what the white man had to offer—novelties, liquor, speed. The Seneca could not make brass kettles, iron axes, guns, or powder. They could weave the fibers of elm and basswood bark, but they could not make the strong cloth of wool that the traders brought.

Every red man wanted what the white man had to sell—his beads, his blankets, his hoes, his hatchets. The Seneca wanted the little mirrors, which were like tiny springs of water that revealed the dirt on a boy's face as well as the paint of the warriors. Mirrors—what wonderful treasures they were! Boys bought mirrors by trading mink or weasel pelts for them, and with mirrors they learned to signal by throwing the reflected sunrays across the landscape. A beam of light from a looking glass could get in one's eyes, too, and blind one for a moment. There were tricks to be done with mirrors.

Traders had such things and Indians could not make

them, but to get them, they would bargain with their hard-won beaverskins. "Just one more pelt," the trader would say, "just one more, and you can have these beads, this blanket, this shining kettle!" To Otetiani a trader was "Mister One-more."

As he wandered through the Indian towns, he saw the havoc that trade had brought to the old way of life. He began to realize that what the traders were urging along with their swapping was something called "civilization" and that the way his own people lived was called "paganism" and "savagery." The smug assurance of the British trader burned into Always Ready's soul, for though he saw much of poverty and cruelty about him in his own people, he saw the same among the pale-faced visitors. He even realized after a time that they did not practice what they preached. Settlers would not keep promises, and when an Indian was murdered, the white man's courts did not punish the culprit.

The Indians detested most the settlers who did not obey the laws of their own government or observe the morality preached by their own clergy. If this civilization was good, why did it not make all white men good? Of course many were honest and kind, but maybe they were forced to be so in order to bait the trap into which the Indians should fall! Suspicions like this began early in the period of contact between Indian and white. Rumor and suspicion became such a part of Otetiani's thinking that he never recovered from their influence. Almost every time he softened in an attempt to see the invading European in a kindlier light, some border culprit would commit an outrage that would send the Indians on war parties of revenge.

He never believed that revenge accomplished its purpose, nor did Old King, whom he loved as a hero.

Indeed, of all the people in Kanadesaga whom Otetiani most admired, Gayengwata, Old King, was foremost. He was a dominant figure and yet a man of the people. He was not really a king, but the name fitted him well. As a sachem he ruled with a flexible rod of justice and looked upon some misdeeds with tolerance, while he punished others with a hand of granite.

Old King had a vast number of friends in faraway places, among them Sir William Johnson, the British superintendent of Indian affairs. Much of the business between Old King and Johnson related to the same French rivalry in trade that had brought about hostility long before 1750. The French wanted trade to veer to the north, and the British quite naturally wanted it to center at Albany and Oswego. To win in this contest, each party lured the Indians with all sorts of trinkets. The Indians, looking to their own advantage, wanted to trade where they would be paid well and they could get goods at the cheapest price. That in the end meant that they traded at British posts.

All this brought about an unhappy state of affairs in which hijacking, robbery of stored skins, and even outright murder were common. The Indians were more than eager to have the wonderful things that came from Europe, and once relying upon them for their needs, they gave up many of their old arts and manufactures. Such trades as pottery making were given up because brass kettles were so much better. Wool cloth, linen sheeting, buttons, needles, thread, china dishes, glass bottles, medicines, and simple chemi-

cals were superior to the products the Indians formerly
had used, and they caused the red men to depend almost
entirely upon the trader's goods. Otetiani saw that to use
things one does not make for himself creates dependence.
The Indians were no longer independent and were losing
their ancient skills and pride along with their old self-
reliance. This dependence began to become irksome and
caused grumbling in every Indian settlement. Some of the
older sachems deplored the changing condition, saying
that the ambitious trader must be checked or all would be
lost.

When Otetiani stepped out of his mother's lodge at the
strawberry thanksgiving festival the very year he had received his name, he saw a great pile of beaverskins being
bartered for a keg of rum.

"Come on, have some," said Burnt Hominy, the village
cynic. "It's good for you."

"Otetiani doesn't get fooled by poison water," the boy
answered.

"Come on, you'll get fooled anyway. They are going to
send a missionary to make us like white folk," taking another swig of rum.

"What is a missionary?" asked Otetiani in alarm.

"You'll find out," was the reply. "Come on before it
gets here! Take some of this. Missionaries? Huh, they come
from the country of the Mohawk nation, and I hear one is
coming pretty soon. The Indians call them 'Black Coats.'"

Otetiani walked away disgusted with what he saw but
suspicious that something called a "missionary" might be
like one of the mystery animals he saw pictured on the

British coat of arms. Yet the sight of the trader tying up packs of pelts for which only rum had been paid made him hope that something drastic might happen to save his people. Maybe the dreaded missionary might help.

When he told a close companion of this hope, he heard only a laugh. Missionaries, he was told, were men who came to make Indians believe what the white man believed. There were three kinds, he learned: the French and two kinds of British, and they didn't like each other but were polite just the same. They carried no guns or rum.

"Did you ever talk to the Mohawk boys who are clerks at the trading post?" asked his friend. "They talk English just like the people from Fort Hunter and Albany. They know what the white people are going to do. One of them told me we must become just as smart as the English and French if we are going to hold our own. He said all of us ought to go to school, learn to read books, and live in houses with plastered walls."

"And must we become like white people?" asked Otetiani.

"Yes, some of us are going to try. I know how to swear already."

"I'll never do it!" exclaimed Otetiani. "I am going to be a Seneca forever! I'll stand by my people as long as I can stand in my moccasins!"

"Remember those Mohawk boys," said his friend, "and see what can happen to boys who read books. They can make marks on paper that mean words. Schools make boys clever, and they learn to make the wonderful articles the traders bring us. Sir William Johnson has a boy he calls

Joseph, and Joseph is the son of a chief named Brant. He has a sister named Molly. They both live like white people and talk English."

"I'll keep my word for all that," replied Otetiani. "The white man shall not destroy the Indian in me, nor shall I let him spoil our way of living."

It was a brave resolution, but a hopeless one, as Otetiani was to learn. Yet he could plainly see that the Indian way was already spoiled and that it was crumbling as the old town once had crumbled. The only remedy was to build anew, but he could not bring himself to believe it.

One thing he could not deny: the white man had come to stay, and he was bound to expand his territory. Even so Otetiani, while wishing to avoid open war, resolved to challenge every step of the intruder's westward march. He would do this as the spokesman of all the red nations, and the white man would be compelled to listen.

[2] *RED JACKET'S HOMELAND*

OTETIANI CAN BE better understood when we catch a
glimpse of the country where he was born—the Finger
Lakes section of central New York State. There long,
clear lakes spread out from the highlands just north of
Pennsylvania and follow rather narrow valleys northward
to a common outlet that flows into the Oswego River and
then into Lake Ontario. The arrangement of these bodies
of water, the Indians told the settlers, suggested that some
master hand had pressed its outstretched fingers upon

19

bedrock and filled the impressions with the waters of many springs.

Seneca Lake is the largest of the five, but there are several smaller lakes hidden between them. There is Owasco, Keuka, Cayuta, and a cluster of "little fingers" farther west. Cayuga Lake is east of Seneca Lake and runs parallel with it, but it is not so long nor deep. There is a small island at its northern end which is the burial ground of a mysterious race of Indians who lived nearby more than two thousand years ago. Seneca Lake, perhaps, has more legends clustering about it than some of the other lakes. The legend of the underwater drums is related still to explain the sound of strange explosions that occur at the lake's bottom at irregular intervals. Canandaigua, the last of the "big fingers," is thought by many to be the most beautiful of all. Seneca myths relate that it was upon the great hill at the southeast end of the lake that their nation's first capitol was built. They also have a legend of a mighty serpent that coiled about another hill and devoured all the people, later disgorging their skulls in the water. Skull-like stones are still found there.

Europeans had seen portions of this country as early as 1615, when Étienne Brulé, a French messenger sent by Samuel de Champlain, crossed its southern reaches. Later the pioneer missionaries of New France came to bring the message of Christianity to the wondering inhabitants. It was not until the soldiers of General John Sullivan came in 1779, however, that the full possibilities of this inland paradise dawned upon the minds of land-hungry white men. But we shall come to that story later.

In this region of varied landscape dwelt the Seneca and

Cayuga nations, brothers and members of the Iroquois confederacy. Their allies, the Mohawk, the Oneida, the Onondaga, and the adopted Tuscarora, lived farther east during Otetiani's youth. The entire group forming the confederacy stretched from the Mohawk Valley near the present city of Schenectady to beyond Skaneateles Lake. The Cayuga had two or three towns and numerous hamlets on or near Cayuga Lake, the westernmost town being Skoiyase, or Long Falls. The thriving village of Waterloo now covers the site. Not far away to the west lived the Seneca, whose towns stretched to the Genesee River and clustered along its banks on both sides.

To the north were the larger lakes, Erie and Ontario, with the surging St. Lawrence arching above as an outlet to the Atlantic Ocean. Bordering all these lakes and waterways were vast areas of forest with frequent regions of open land called prairies, or oak openings. There were wide valleys to the north of the Finger Lakes, great level, fertile areas suitable for agriculture, enormous swamps, and a region of small, gravelly hills called drumlins. In some of the rich lands cleared by beavers, forest fires, or nature, there were farming lands where the Seneca and their brethren cultivated their own varieties of corn, beans, and squash along with native tobacco, sunflowers, and artichokes.

When the first sharp rivalry between the French and the English for valuable furs had subsided in this region, most of the Indian hunters seeking a hopeful market went south into Pennsylvania or north into Canada, where the conquered Huron country still had enough furs to serve a limited trade. Central New York by the time Otetiani was born had been hunted until fur-bearing animals had become almost extinct, but deer were to be found in a seemingly unlimited quantity.

Here, then, was a land that invited living creatures, which, when hunted sparingly, could be found in vast abundance. Their trails could be seen throughout the eastern woodlands, and quite naturally men seeking food, adventure, and a new homeland followed the ready-made roads of the animals. The outcome after one group of tribes had made their settlements was that other tribes came, saw, and sought to conquer. Central New York, or Kanonah, as the Indians called it, was perhaps the most fought-for region on the continent north of Mexico. It was a region that had almost every natural advantage. To see the broad beaver meadows and grassy valleys, the myriads of waterfalls, and swift-running streams was to covet ownership with an overpowering passion; and that passion always meant war. Last of the native peoples to conquer it were the Seneca, who either drove out or absorbed their predecessors of many years before.

The Seneca were the westernmost of a great stream of migrants which we now call the Iroquois. They may have been descendants of the mound-building nations that had occupied Ohio and then, for some unknown reason, had fled. In changing homelands, they had abandoned many of their ancient ways of doing things. A prophet who cried that they must flee from destruction may have appeared, or drought and starvation may have driven them out. But in Otetiani's time the Iroquois tribes and nations, together with the people called the Wyandot, or Huron, held the new land on both sides of Lake Erie and Lake Ontario and made the land blossom wherever their towns and plantations were established.

At first these energetic migrants sought the high hills as places of refuge because there were other tribes to be absorbed or expelled. Not until the year 1500 was the region made secure for the nations of the Iroquois, among whom the Seneca were the most populous. To add to population, they invited captive groups and surrounding tribes not of their blood or language to unite with them in peaceful cooperation. It was an original Americanization scheme, and by it the Iroquois grew in numbers until few enemies were willing to challenge their warriors in battle.

The villages of the Seneca and Cayuga, like those of their brother Onondaga, Oneida, and Mohawk, at first. were walled by tree trunks stuck in embankments surrounded by outer ditches. These kept enemies from getting inside and discouraged hungry wolves, with which the forest abounded.

Houses were of several types, but the ordinary dwelling was a structure called a long house. This building was sometimes two hundred feet long and was divided into several compartments, one for each family living within. The cooking fires were built on the sanded floor, and the smoke ascended, when it would, through large rectangular openings in the arched roof. A village was composed of several long houses, often as many as a hundred but usually not over fifty. There were also smaller houses and sometimes individual cabins. The small house, however, was usually in a camp or along the trails between villages. Sometimes it was occupied by a lonely family, and sometimes it was a free stopping place with a well-stocked larder and piles of wood for fuel. All that was required was that the temporary guest replenish the shelves and chop more wood. It was a guest house for all who required rest and food.

In time, as European traders and explorers discovered this snugly furnished domain, other kinds of houses were built, and gable roofs came into vogue. The more ancient long house was made by erecting an ingenious framework of large poles and then placing big sheets of elm, white cedar, or chestnut bark over the wooden skeleton. Inside along the wall were wide benches or bunks, seven or eight feet long and about four feet wide. These shelves served as seats by day and as beds at night. A neatly sewed curtain, sometimes painted on the underside, was hung from a pole above the benches. At night it could be dropped down, making a comfortable berth like that of a modern Pullman car. In fact there was also an upper berth where clothing and baggage could be stored or, in a pinch, where children could be stowed away amid soft furs.

When Europeans began to wander through the Iroquois settlements, they found twelve large towns, some of which were well stockaded. In sheltered valleys they also found smaller hamlets where a few families lived by permission of the sachems of the great towns.

As the quest of the French, Dutch, and English continued after 1615, the Indians who supplied pelts began to establish more and more of these little villages. Finally only a few of the older settlements had populations of more than five or six hundred persons.

The demand for fine furs, especially beaver, developed a new drive among the Iroquois. It was to get from other tribes by exchange, purchase, or pillage all the furs they could lay hands upon and to sell them in the highest market. In other words, they wanted to be the middlemen and to control the fur trade at the source of supply. To do this, they waged bloody wars and in the end triumphed. By military strategy they defeated an Indian population in eastern America of a hundred thousand people with an army of not more than two thousand men. In this way they had broken down all effective competition and had emerged in 1650 as just about the most important Indians on the whole continent. It was then that both the British and the French tried to win their friendship and alliance. The Europeans showered the Indians with gifts, medals, clothing, and ornaments. But presents did not buy friendship for long. Trade advantage and access to raw material guided the loyalties of the Iroquois. Thus at times they appeared to be uncertain allies, shifting from the French to the British and, after the American Revolution, largely to the Americans. "Safety begins at home" was their principle. Their experience with other national powers seemed to show that the nation that does not take care of itself cannot deal advantageously with others. This principle was one that Otetiani learned early in his youth, and he held to it throughout his life.

Because of the profits to be derived from furs, Iroquois hunters wandered to faraway places and of necessity largely abandoned their former centralized village life and an agricultural economy. Under pressure for large quantities of pelts, they spent most of their time hunting instead of tilling their great cornlands. To carry on large-scale fur traffic in preference to raising food was a backward step. It contributed to the downfall of the eastern Indians and to the weakening of the Iroquois. The latter had hunted in their agricultural days, but the hunting was for the purpose of fulfilling their own needs. It was not, like the later fur hunting and trapping, devoted to the satisfaction of a market as enormous as all Europe.

In a dim way, because they had become accustomed to hunting for competing markets, the Iroquois sensed a change for the worse. But through this change they thought they had hope for a new future, a future entrusted to the white providers of axes, kettles, knives, cloth, and beads. The vital question was whether or not in their altered way of life, with its growing dependence upon the goods that the white traders brought, they could develop new strength. Could the Indians become strong and more independent by abandoning their old utensils and taking the new? This was a question that troubled several Indian leaders. Among them was Pontiac, who declared that no more white men's goods should be used; only home-made native products should be employed. Pontiac's plan failed because evolution does not work that way.

By 1759 the trade rivalry between France and England had brought about a most perplexing situation for the Iroquois. They would have liked to be friendly with both nations and at the same time to sell their furs to the highest bidder. The two European nations were thrown into such commercial conflict that the Great Fur War (which we call the French and Indian War) broke out, control of the pelt trade being the object. The Indians shifted their loyalty from side to side as best suited their own interests; but at last the powerful Iroquois gave all-out support to the English. Then Niagara, Quebec, and Montreal fell. The French had been defeated.

[3] *LISTENING AND LEARNING*
AT SENECA CASTLE

WITH AN OLD GUN that the trading-post blacksmith had
repaired for him, Otetiani hunted the marshes north of
Seneca and Cayuga lakes. Ducks were plentiful, and deer
were to be found in the uplands south of all the lakes.
Otetiani was fond of hunting, but he enjoyed his long
walks most, for they gave him time to think and to practice replies he could make to questions if he were ever
asked. He wanted to be "always ready," and "Be prepared" was one of his mottoes.

However wonderful the outer world appeared, Kanadesaga was a castle of dreams where the world of the
Seneca became acquainted with the wonders of what the
white man brought. At Kanadesaga there was a man who
made implements of iron and mended hoes and shovels.
There was another who made nails and could put timbers
together with spikes. He could cut a log into thin strips
and make boards and squared beams, and he had a two-
handled knife that he called a "drawshave."

Officers of the British king came to talk to the inspec-
tor of traders. These men from afar wore gold chains
and gold braid; they had long coats and scarves of silk.
They devoted much time to writing in books and counting
things.

Otetiani knew that these men were British and that
even the British had their tribes; one was called Scottish,
and its men were pleasant to deal with. They were almost
like the French, but they didn't like Indians quite so well
as did the Frenchmen. It was not hard to learn from the
interpreter that these men were always afraid of something and that they kept the town under guard at all
times. Was it the French that they feared? Whatever it
was they feared, it was in Sir William Johnson's mind, no
doubt, when he caused a blockhouse to be built in the
very center of Kanadesaga. Its heavy walls of hewn timbers were proof against tomahawks and bullets. When it
was built, the Seneca made no objection to this token of
British power or to the fact that no French trader was
welcome there.

The Indians made many jokes about the fort and
laughed because the British had expected to place a gar-

rison there. When all was ready, however, the Seneca refused to allow troops to come. Old King spoke out against such an obvious seizure of territory. "We're friends now," he declared. "Let's stay friends, and we'll manage the fort."

Burnt Hominy, the town's rogue and gloomiest pessimist, would laugh as he looked at the massive building.

"Ho, ho, hoh!" he would explode. "Here's where the British were fooled!"

"If we fooled them, is the fort now ours?" asked Otetiani.

"Always was! Hah! We'll teach those traders from the Mohawk Valley that we can run our own business. Listen, Otetiani," he went on to say, "here's a secret—we will even take care of the British at Niagara very soon. Farmer's Brother, our chief warrior, is going to challenge the British with a big band of fighting men from the Genesee towns. We'll see who owns the Niagara River and its roads!"

Otetiani was distressed at this news because he thought there might be a better way to settle a dispute than by shooting. The British were friends—very smug friends— he thought, but their smugness was no excuse for fighting. Indians always lost in the end when they fought against overwhelming odds.

One day, not long after Burnt Hominy's prediction, a runner dashed into Kanadesaga to relate the story of a terrible fight at Devil's Hole on the Niagara River where a road runs near a high cliff. Farmer's Brother, the runner said, had lost control of one of his bands of young warriors. They were mad with the lust for revenge and lashed their horses against an English wagon train, driving men, horses, cattle, and wagons over the cliff to perish on the sharp rocks below. Only two or three escaped, one a drummer boy whose drum strap caught on a broken limb far down the bank.

"Sir William, my friend, will be furious about this," Old King exclaimed. "If I know the British, they will not take a licking of this kind without making us pay in blood."

Old King was right, for the officers of the crown demanded the culprit warriors as the price of peace. Failure to deliver them would mean war. Farmer's Brother was not blamed, because he had tried to restrain the hotheaded men. The leaders were turned over to the British and hanged as a lesson to others.

Otetiani, who loved the Niagara region and had once visited its fort and the falls and cave under the cataract, pondered this proof of British power. They not only hanged the fighting men who had whipped them but had demanded the ownership of the road as well and got it. Did this mean that the British had some power by which they could forgive their own sins while exacting penalties from others? The Keepers of the Faith had talked over this question and had decided that power came from wanting things very much and then inventing them or taking them away from others. "It is better to want little and love one's neighbors," they said. But Otetiani saw clearly that not knowing and not wanting kept people very poor and uncomfortable.

Very many religious white men thought along the same lines, though they expressed the thought differently. Some had strong convictions about all kinds of wrongdoing. One of these was a young man named Samuel Kirkland. He felt the call to go forth and preach to the distant Iroquois, who, he learned, were called Seneca. Thus, from across the reaches of western Massachusetts, Samuel Kirkland, though not yet ordained as a minister, prepared to answer his call to the service of humanity. He knew something about the fight at Devil's Hole and realized that it was the protest of men who felt they had no other means of gaining attention to their plight. Kirkland wanted to make these same men and their kindred aware of the power of a great religion that would help them find a better way of life.

Thus, later in the winter after the Devil's Hole episode, Kirkland left his home and set out on a journey to the residence of Sir William Johnson. He wanted the super-intendent's permission to visit the Seneca people of Kana-desaga.

Superintendent Johnson was cordial, but he was careful to say that he did not recommend such a visit at that time. Kirkland, however, would not be daunted by winter's cold or the long walk in deep snow. With two Seneca guides he made the trip in twenty-one days, eating cold food like a wolf and sleeping rolled up in a thin blanket on the snow.

Arriving at Kanadesaga, he was welcomed by Old King, who looked over the credentials and recommendations of Sir William. At last a missionary had come, and as Ote-tiani peered through the cracks in the council house wall, he saw that the missionary was really a man and not a horse with a horn. Otetiani had no opinion yet about the stranger; but Burnt Hominy was sure that the white man was a wizard in disguise, who might turn into a wolf or a crow and fly over the houses spreading death powder. Otetiani doubted this when he heard the missionary's speech explaining his purpose in coming. Surely the man meant no harm; nor did he carry a gun or sword.

Old King, convinced that Sir William had truthfully represented the young missionary, gave Kirkland his hand and adopted him as a son. He told the people in the council that protection must be given the young man and that respect and courtesy were expected under the penalty of heavy censure.

Burnt Hominy, however, was not so easily convinced. He said that he felt sure that the missionary would bring calamity and death, "just as the French missionaries years ago had done."

A few days after his adoption Kirkland was given a home with a kindly-disposed family. The man was mild and obliging to the missionary, and the wife was a good cook and neat. All was well for several days, during which the missionary picked up many words. When callers came in for a closer inspection, he would point at objects and say, "*Naote?*" The word meant, "What's that?"

In this way he learned that *jeeyaa* was dog; *ganohsote,* house; *yeoh,* woman; *otoeweh,* cold; *ohodieyeh,* hot. Sometimes he would mispronounce a word, which made the boys listening at the doorway laugh so hard that they would roll in the snow. A slight difference in pronunciation could make a word mean something entirely different.

As the red men watched the missionary trying to learn the Seneca tongue and to act as an Indian, they recalled the medicine man's story of how the human race was created. The story related that the Creator simply wanted to make one kind of man-creature and so molded clay into a human form and baked it. But the baking was too long, and the man had turned entirely black. He tried again, using less time and a lighter fire. He failed again, for the product was white and easily crumbled. With a final effort he baked his molded figure midway between the others, producing a man with a beautiful skin of reddish-brown. It was the Indian, the perfect man! "White man too white," the storytellers laughed. "Now white man spends all his time trying to be like us so that he will look brown. He likes to live outdoors, to hunt and fish, and, watch out, soon he will want all of our country."

Kirkland listened to many tales like this, as had other settlers. He took them with a smile and asked for more. He could not tell a story in the native tongue yet, but he did try to use Seneca words. For instance, when he tried to tell the women who came into the house that the corn was ripe, pointing to a string of corn hanging from the ceiling, the younger women would titter gleefully. He blushed when he learned that he actually had said, "I love you," instead.

Progress in learning was rapid, however, and for three days he busied himself making lists of words and trying to pronounce them. His host was helpful but often seemed to be thinking of something far away. Then the wife came to his rescue but cautioned Kirkland not to pronounce a word the way the boys recommended; it might mean some wicked thing. Naughty boys were forever whispering strange words and pointing to something to which the words did not apply.

All was going smoothly notwithstanding the mischief

of the boys, and the people were beginning to like their new brother. He liked the people, too. He felt assured that he would succeed in his mission.

On the night of the fourth day in his new dwelling place, he was awakened by the sound of heavy sobbing.

"What's the matter?" he called out in the darkness, springing up in his bed and opening the curtain.

"My husband——" came the cry, "my husband, he's dead!"

For a few minutes Kirkland felt stunned. The terrible fear that he might be accused of killing his host filled his mind. Getting a grip on himself, he hurriedly dressed and went to the sorrowing widow, endeavoring to comfort her. Relatives were sent for, and they soon arrived, pouring out questions and uttering moans. "He has never known illness," the widow said. "He appeared well yesterday."

The next morning the death cry, *"Goweh!"* was sounded from the door of the house of sorrow, and a runner sped through the town crying the news.

When the hostile warriors heard of this strange death, Burnt Hominy began to shout that the missionary was a wizard and had caused the unexpected sorrow. "He has poisoned him," he cried.

When Kirkland understood what had been said, he was approached by Old King who took his hand and said, "Let your mind be at ease," and he smiled. "We'll place you in the blockhouse where you will be out of the lodge of sorrow; it will be more comfortable."

Once in the blockhouse, however, wild yells were heard outside. The hotheads, who had opened a keg of rum, were shouting threats that Kirkland knew might be carried out if hands could be laid upon him. Under cover of darkness, Kirkland was led by friendly Indians far out into the forest and hidden in a sap house, where no one lived except during maple-sugar time.

With danger all about him, he still insisted in praising the Lord by singing in his loudest voice. His guarding friends looked at each other with astonishment. Such noises certainly would be recognized by prowlers, and harm might follow.

"No, no," cautioned the wife of his guard. "We have heard you sing many times before, and we'd love to hear you again; but not now, not now!"

The guard nodded in agreement, and Kirkland toned down his voice but continued his psalm. The Indian hefted his gun and looked at the powder pan. It was all right to sing, but it was just as well to back up prayers with a good gun.

The next day food came, and even a paper of salt was provided. It was known that white brothers liked salt with their meats. Better still was the news that an inquest had been held, the wife's testimony taken, and proof offered that Kirkland had not blown poison in the air or done any other harmful thing. The hotheads were sour at this decision, but the missionary was delighted. He thanked the news bringers and heard them reply, "Old King has powerful words."

Coming back to the village and entering the council house to thank his adopted father, he saw Old King's face light up with a smile as he said, "All is now peaceful; fear not."

All this was a lesson to Otetiani, who eagerly absorbed

the teachings of the nation's leaders. Yet, as he watched the events of the Kirkland incident, he knew only too well that a peaceful man when aroused can become a dangerous foe. What could this man Kirkland become should he have cause to be fired with anger?

But, no matter what mischief was done him, the missionary did not show anger or fear. When tormented, he would burst forth in song and his face would light up with a smile. Such a man was beyond suspicion.

Trying to satisfy the missionary's curiosity, the Seneca invited him to the long house where their winter rites of thanksgiving were held. He saw the dances, heard the songs, and witnessed the strange ceremonies conducted by men in feather-decked costumes. Among these was a ceremony performed by dancers wearing masks. They were medicine men believed to represent creatures who were on earth before true mankind was created.

Otetiani watched the missionary but spoke to him rarely. This does not mean that he asked no questions about him. He did, learning many things about the good man. Throughout his life, however, Otetiani wondered if, good as they are, missionaries do not cause trouble. He was sure that they did, but others were just as sure that they brought good fortune. Long did this problem trouble his mind, but he never quite solved it. Missionaries may be good, he thought, but they want us to give up our beliefs. He felt that he could not do that.

Kirkland at last departed from Kanadesaga, called away by other duties. One of them was the founding of a school for Oneida Indian boys. Since then it has come to be known as Hamilton College. Many years passed before

Otetiani, who had become Chief Sagoyewatha, meaning "He keeps them awake," saw the missionary again. The chief found that Kirkland had grown strong and commanding in appearance. He had become a noted minister and educator, and he served as chaplain in the army of General Sullivan when the latter, as we shall see, was ordered to punish the Seneca and Cayuga and finally to burn Kanadesaga, Otetiani's castle of dreams.

Meanwhile Kirkland had learned to speak the Iroquois dialects fluently, and hundreds of Indians had become his devoted friends. This was especially true of the Oneida and Tuscarora people, but to the end Otetiani distrusted the motives of missionaries. That the lives of those who listened to them became changed, he could not deny. But they no longer seemed to be Indians; neither were they like white men.

Kirkland was not the first white man to stay at Kanadesaga, and he was not the last. The missionary's visit, however, was one of the most important events in Otetiani's life. It helped shape his attitudes throughout his career and built up an influence that he fought to the day of his death.

[4] *A LAND OF NO RESTRAINT*

THE BORDER BETWEEN the land of the whites and the Indians was tomahawk country during the youthful days of
Otetiani. Like thousands of other boys, he saw shouting
young men go forth to war and some return with wounds
that made them cripples for life. He wondered if tribes
of mankind ever could have peace and security, and he
remembered how the older men always counseled peace
unless invasions came.

Few young warriors of the Seneca, however, were as
patient as their elders, and most wanted to join raiding
parties to punish the settlers for their forays against Indian villages. This forbidden fighting, often accompanied

ɔy massacre, worried the sachems and made them cautious. With hotheaded war chiefs, who would not submit to restraint, revenge and face saving were major motives. And then war meant adventure and excitement; everybody wanted excitement.

Sir William Johnson, who knew all these things, was a most patient man who disliked to bother his London superiors. Nevertheless, he found it necessary to report how the Indians felt. Well did he know that lawless bordermen violated every solemn promise crown agents had made and had struck again and again at Indian villages, looting where they could.

"On this and every other subject for grievance," the Seneca chiefs had complained to him, "we have patiently waited for redress for years, and now we are quite tired. We begin to despair that all [other] nations, becoming impatient, cannot restrain their warriors."

Such was the report made by Sir William to the Earl of Hillsborough, crown officer in London. Nor was the earl insensible to the complaints of Sir William. He knew that the king had given the colonies the right to make regulations concerning Indian commerce but that nothing had been done. This was a bitter fact. Deploring the unhappy state of affairs, he addressed all colonial governors, including those in Canada where there was little trouble, "As the Indians have in the strongest manner expressed their impatience under abuses to which they are constantly exposed, the King has commanded me to signify his pleasure that you, without delay, fall upon some measures of putting Indian affairs under such regulations as may . . . prevent abuses of the trade and those violences and encroachments of the frontier inhabitants of which the Indians so justly complain."

This order, after it had been communicated to the governors, was read and explained to the Indians. Otetiani, as a courier for Old King, heard the explanation. The Indians were convinced that it was not the government, the king, or his agents who were wronging them. It was the settlers, who would not submit to the law. Otetiani was impressed by this fact, for he saw in it both the inability of the king and his agents to restrain outlawry and the stubborn will of the pale-faced race to conquer when opportunity offered the chance.

On every side Otetiani heard the war chiefs cry out, "If the king cannot control his people, why should we not take up the hatchet in revenge?"

This was the question that troubled Kanadesaga, whose warriors were held in check by the flinty fist of Old King. But he, too, was becoming angry at the almost daily reports of the murder of his kinsmen. The irony of the situation burned deeper and deeper into the heart of Otetiani, who heard white men say, "The land is destined to be the property of civilized men and not the hunting ground of savages who make no decent use of it." At every council and at every gathering of settlers, Otetiani heard the interpreter translate the half-whispered remarks of men who grimly set their jaws and determined to flout the orders of a king who knew nothing of the land hunger of his subjects.

It was during this period of tension, when one civilization was cracking down upon the other, that the family of Chief Logan of the wandering Mingo tribes in Pennsylvania was massacred by lawless bordermen. It made no difference to these settlers whether an Indian were friend or foe. Logan, said to have been a relative of Otetiani's father, was a Cayuga. He had been placed on the Susquehanna River as the Iroquois representative in charge of hunting bands and wandering groups of displaced Indians. He was considered one of the noblest of his people. Indeed, he was one of Otetiani's heroes, for he was both a warrior and a counselor. His orations were strong arguments for peace with the whites. But now Logan's family had been slain by lawless men.

The Indians found it difficult to understand the hate of some of the border people, forgetting that revenge breeds reprisal. Logan may have forgotten, too. Following the loss of his family, though long called by the Indians "the white man's friend," he mustered his warriors and attacked white settlements, shrieking as he scalped his victims like other savage warriors. In the end he was defeated and brought to bay.

It was the very grimness of the conflict between two races that gnawed at the heart of Otetiani, now a stalwart young man of twenty-four. He had listened to many stirring accounts of his people's suffering from unjust attack. He knew of Logan's oratory and, impressed by the power of words, sought to emulate his distinguished kinsman. Logan's tragedy was an important factor in conditioning the thinking of Otetiani.

As a budding orator now, for he had spoken in the tribal council, Otetiani's problem was to get results without bringing ridicule upon himself when he practiced his art.

To escape the watchful eyes of his associates, he traveled southward along the west side of Seneca Lake, crossed the deep gullies with their astonishing waterfalls, and camped at Catherine's Town. Moodily pacing the slatey shelves along the glen at Montour Falls, he would plan his speeches and then, in measured sentences and modulated voice, would try to speak as no Seneca had ever spoken before. He tried to make his thoughts clear and pointed and to clothe them with words that would crash into the minds of his hearers. He taught himself to say, "My brothers, lend me your ears," in tones that would stir the listener and move him to wonder.

He learned to analyze a subject and then to express his ideas about it in words that conjured up pictures of fact and fancy. He taught himself to measure his sentences like the words of a song and to deliver them with a force that struck home. It was this achievement in rhetoric that his unskilled interpreters confessed they were unable to reproduce in the frontier English that they had at their command. Every listener, however, whether he understood Seneca or not, reacted to the cadence of his voice, its smoothness, its rhythm, and the reasoning behind it. When he practiced speaking, the steady drone of the waterfalls deepened his voice as he competed with the roar of the water. He developed his tones so that they became vibrant and penetrating.

Often his eyes were dreamy when he returned to Catherine's Town, and even when he went back to Kanadesaga, he spoke little except to Old King and his mother.

"You are much away from me," she would gently chide

him. "What is my son doing in French Catherine's town?"

It was the quiet rebuke of a middle-aged woman needing a son's care.

Otetiani had a ready excuse, and with his eye flashing he would reply. "I was at Montour Falls," he would answer, "Loganing!"

Then he would seize his hunting gun, scout for game, and shortly return with food for the empty shelf. Once again Blue Flower would have meat with her hominy.

It was now 1774. Events were moving rapidly. Between the incursions of bordermen and the rash action of young warriors, there was much unrest. Yet Otetiani never took part in these bloody raids, believing that war only invited counter-reprisal.

In the Mohawk Valley another Iroquois (whom his people called Thayendanegea, and whom the British called Joseph Brant) was rising as a leader. Unlike Otetiani, however, Joseph was the son of a recognized leader. He was also the grandson of a chief who had led the French against the Seneca in 1687, causing the loss of all their great towns by fire.

Joseph Brant, as he had been baptized, was a close friend of Sir William, and after the forest fashion Sir William had married his sister Molly. It was a happy alliance, too, for it brought the loyalties of the Mohawk to the British and swung them to an out-and-out espousal of the crown. No more would Mohawk chiefs listen to the allurements of French traders.

The Mohawk people had known a great deal about French missionaries, who had suffered much in their efforts to enlighten the Indians. These same Mohawks later came to understand that most of the English had a faith different from that of the French. This difference of religion was puzzling to the Indians, who began to wonder at Kirkland's plain preaching and lack of ceremony. Kirkland was a strong influence among the Oneida and Tuscarora. His school, the Oneida Academy was training Indian boys in new ideas of liberty and civilization. The Mohawk, loving Sir William Johnson, liked his Anglican Church best, and would sit in the pews and sing "God Save the King." Kirkland's theme was "God save the people."

There was a gap between all sects, and the Seneca, few of whom were yet Christians, wondered why. Otetiani, who pondered the lack of full accord among the churches, never forgot his initial shock at their lack of harmony. He said, "What is the matter? Why don't they agree since they have the same book?"

As a courier Otetiani carried messages into most British outposts and forts, especially those along the Great Lakes. In these strongholds he became a familiar figure. Among his own people along the Genesee, likewise, he seemed a brilliant and promising young man, though he seemed to be a bit vain. In his own mind was the hope that someday he might become one of the sachems of the nation.

As a boy he had learned that the chief matrons of each of the eight clans in his nation (Turtle, Wolf, Bear, Beaver, Snipe, Deer, Heron, and Hawk) held the power of nominating and removing sachems. He knew that a sachem could not go to war without vacating his office, because the Iroquois government was dedicated to the preservation of peace. He believed in peace but saw that war sometimes was hard to avoid. "Our fathers are right in opposing war," he declared. "Because they are right, I'll not join the hostile bands beyond the Ohio River."

"Are you a coward?" an arrogant war captain asked. "Why don't you fight like a man?"

"I fight for the Great Peace," he would declare. "Is it wrong to fight for what is right?"

Whatever the irate hotheads thought of Otetiani, they could not answer that pointed question, for it was the basis of their ancient law.

More and more, as he was taunted by his own generation, Otetiani's determination deepened. He would stand inflexibly for the ancient faith. Little did he then realize that time might create new needs and that a new pattern must be woven over the older warp to meet a changed world.

However this may have been, it now became apparent that the Weaver of Patterns in human society was trying out new stitches in the colony of Massachusetts. Colonists were having trouble with British authorities there, and most of the other colonies were quite sympathetic with the rebelling people of Boston. There had been trouble before over a shipload of tea, and the blood of shouting, rebellious Bostonians had stained the common. The trouble now seemed even more serious, for rebellion against the king seemed imminent. Sir William, when he heard the rumors, was much distressed. If the revolt were to spread, he knew that it would attract to his valley settlers who had defied him and called him a "tyrant." He wanted no skirmishes with his neighbors, but he took the precaution to have soldiers where they could be quickly summoned to guard his property.

When the grapevine of the forest flashed the startling rumor that resistance would openly break out, British authorities were alerted and so were such stalwarts of liberty as Nicholas Herkimer and Samuel Kirkland.

Over the Six Nations, however, loomed the towering form of Joseph Brant. He boldly avowed his loyalty to the crown, for it had ever been loyal to him. Settlers? Had they any rights at all when they defied the law? Did they not enjoy freedom only to abuse it? How did they employ their liberties except to flout the orders of Sir William and the commands of their king? Such were Brant's questions about his white neighbors, though he was on friendly terms with many of them.

At this very moment of stress, the Indians were demanding relief from the depredations of settlers who had invaded the Ohio country. The very presence of Iroquois settlements along the Ohio River meant friction with white men who also wanted to live there, despite treaties that reserved the land for the Indians. Sir William tried to induce the Indians of his superintendency to return to their homes in the Finger Lakes and Genesee country, thus relieving the tension of the border. Some of the Seneca bands accepted the orders of Sir William, but others refused to do so.

In an effort to bring about an understanding, therefore, the superintendent summoned a grand council to be held in June, 1774. To it came more than six hundred Iroquois delegates. Few thought that they were deserving of punishment for their own actions against the whites.

On the other hand, they were highly sensitive about the wrongs inflicted upon them. Many innocent parties had been punished, they affirmed.

There were many speeches at this council. Both sides were frank in their statements, but British officials were embarrassed because they had little defense for the lawless acts of their settlers. Yet British officers had done their best to curb the raids of both Indians and frontiersmen. In answer to Sir William's invitation a Seneca chief opened the case for his nation, addressing Sir William in a sad tone. "Your people are ungovernable," he said. "Perhaps they are more so than ours. They seem to despise your orders and disregard the promises of their government. When they trespass on our Ohio lands, they say they will do as they please."

The chief then looked at Sir William as if he were now compelled to make a last threat before his people took to arms. "If this is the case," he said, "we must look upon every promise made to us as of no value. If you have the authority you claim, we hope you will restrain your people and make them obey. Otherwise——"

His appeal was based upon the agreement between the whites and the Indians that the Ohio River should form the western boundary line of the colonies, and upon this the Indians firmly insisted. They failed to understand that a mighty wave of immigration was about to break upon them, which, despite laws, treaties, or promises to them, would engulf the west country. Nothing could stop it. Only a few wiser Indians saw that the migration was inevitable. The white man wanted land, homes, freedom, and power over the soil. Yet the Indians, wise or foolish, ignorant or informed, sought to defer the day of invasion. They stubbornly wanted to hold their own and live their lives undisturbed.

On July 11, 1774, after trying to soothe the Indians and to calm their resentments, Sir William was prostrated by the intense heat of the day but wearily carried on. He thanked the delegates for their assurances of loyalty and friendship and then mentioned the boundary-jumping problem.

"Brothers," he said in a tired voice, "I am sorry to hear of the encroachments of some of our people [English] of whom you have so often complained. This you may be assured is without the knowledge or consent of the government; and the king will take measures to prevent [further] intrusion."

Ignorant and rebellious frontiersmen had committed irregularities, he admitted. He thought, however, that certain southern tribes had, by their own conduct, aroused the anger of the settlers. Nevertheless, promised Sir William Johnson, "These men will be sought after and punished."

A Cayuga speaker now introduced the subject of the rum trade, urging government control of irresponsible traders. To this Sir William replied by recommending that the traders be ejected by the Indians themselves. At every step the superintendent seemed to evade the question, making excuses and promising results in the future. The Indians glowered with darkened faces and began to murmur.

Sir William even yet tried to promise relief and in a faltering manner admitted the abuses of misguided men.

He could hardly speak now and in a husky voice called for his brother-in-law Chief Joseph Brant, making one final appeal for more patience.

"Joseph, Joseph, control your people!" he whispered. "Control your——"

But the distressed superintendent said no more. He only choked and, aided by his attendants, was assisted to the house. Soon his heavy breathing ceased. Sir William Johnson, His Majesty's superintendent, was dead.

There was consternation when the news was announced. The Indians realized that a giant had fallen, and at Johnson Hall his successors realized that there was no easy solution for the current tangled situation.

To the Mohawk and Seneca the question was whether they should take sides in case of an open outbreak of the colonists against Britain. Would it be better to remain neutral? Possibly so. But what about their agreements to support the British? Could some nations of the Iroquois declare war and others remain neutral? Plainly not, for their government was dedicated to lasting peace, and all warfare waged by their short-tempered young men was contrary to the policy of the League of the Iroquois. If now there was indecision on the part of the Indians, doubt soon disappeared. Even Otetiani now saw that a firm stand must be taken.

It was Molly Brant, who now raised her voice to utter an opinion and a challenge, who stung her people to action. "Hesitate? Why? Who was your most loyal friend? Who, on the other hand, killed your women and children? Who protected them? Where now is your manhood and courage? Fight, fight in the name of Sir William!"

The die was cast, but Otetiani saw no hope for his people if they joined in a war against the American colonists. Tactfully he warned his tribesmen that the honest men among the Americans would be compelled to muster their forces against the king and all his allies, and these included the Iroquois. The settlers had been roused to resistance, and that meant bloodshed. It was fight now or back down. In the light of what had happened, how could the Iroquois back down?

[5] *THE RUMBLE*
OF DISTANT THUNDER

OTETIANI BY 1774 was a young man of twenty-four years
and of growing reputation in the world of the Iroquois.
Though considered a bit vain and overeager to be known
as a candidate for a chief's position, he was so fast becoming a master of debate that the older people began
to look to him and say, "There is a youth of great promise!"

One day, during the period when he was basking in the
good will of his elders, he was walking the paths of the
village of Canawaugus. He came upon two men who were
sitting just outside the council lodge talking about affairs

at Allegany. One of them was tall; the other was thin and
unhealthy looking. When Otetiani came along the path, the
tall man stood up to bar the way.

"So it is Otetiani who knows so much about the old
days!" he exclaimed, his olive skin becoming crimson. "So
you think you could talk the people into being strong
again! *Chisnah!* You are too young even to think about
what your elders should do."

"What have I said now?" asked Otetiani, wondering at
the wrath of his clansman.

"You have said too much," was the answer. "You are too
young to talk so boldly about what the people should do."

"I always supposed that truth could be told even by a
child," answered Otetiani. "What has age to do with recognizing facts?"

"You will be recognizing facts if you don't keep your
silence," sternly said the tall man; but the thin man only
glowered, his face dark and scowling.

"Well, maybe I'll be a sachem someday," answered
Otetiani. "Then I can speak as I wish."

"You will never be a sachem of the long house!" fairly
exploded the thin man. "You are too forward, too sure of
yourself."

"What have you to say about what I shall be?" asked
Otetiani.

"My brother is the newly chosen candidate," answered
the tall man. "He will have much to say when the time
comes as to who shall be a civil ruler."

The thin man still frowned. "You are not qualified," he
spat. "You are of an unknown family—your mother is not
of the name-bearing families. Your father——"

"My father was a good man," answered Otetiani, breathing rapidly and clenching his fists.

"Not good enough," answered the thin man.

"See here!" exclaimed the tall man. "I am the war captain of this nation. My brother Handsome Lake will be the great sachem. You are nothing. *Seegwah!*" "*Seegwah*" was the word used to send a dog away, and Otetiani flared at the insult.

"I'll be a sachem of the league if it kills me!" he boasted. "In time I will expose your skulking deceit. War captain indeed! You are the captain of your own wampum pouch!"

The tall man glared now and walked toward Otetiani. "Remember this," said he. "So long as you live, you will never be permitted to take the high office of sachem. I said, 'So long as you live.' You may be buried at any time. I do not wish to hear any more from you."

"You will hear more from me," promised Otetiani walking away.

Youthful and impetuous, he had made two bitter enemies, and now he must watch for some sudden shot or hidden trap that would lay him low. But why watch? The enemy who is wise never tells what he will do or when. Even then, when an enemy shoots, however strong his bow, his arrows must be straight. Otetiani knew that the arrows of the tall man and the thin man were not straight, and he was not afraid.

Years after, the tall man became the great Cornplanter, and the thin man became Handsome Lake the Prophet. Both were powerfully placed, and both were wary of Otetiani's penetrating mind, sharp words, and cutting sarcasm. As we shall see, Otetiani was to hear from them again.

The problem now with the young man was to make good his ambition to hold high office. Could he cultivate the tribal authorities who were the name givers? Could he please the women of the clan to the extent of securing a nomination? There was just one barrier, but he did not know that it could harm him; he was too far advanced in his thinking for the common crowd. Moreover, he had too much assurance and wit. Sachems of the Six Nations must be humble, self-effacing men, and Otetiani was anything but inconspicuous as a youth or later.

Such is the tradition of how Always Ready first aroused the antagonism of the two great men at Allegany. Thereafter he was a marked man with bitter enemies. But he also had warm supporters.

During his visits to the hidden world of his own people, Otetiani had discovered the charm of the valley of the Genesee and had visited all of its hamlets northward from Caneadea and the deep gorge settlements at Gardeau to Canawaugus. The towns of the French-loving Seneca at Nunda and Dansville were known to him, too, and there he had observed the fierceness of their young warriors. At Squakie Hill, where the.adopted Mesquakie lived, and at Coreorgonel on Cayuga Lake, he had seen how adopted people thrived. Of all places, however, he best loved the Genesee Valley, where the deep soil and numerous cleared spaces could be tilled with ease.

Roving from the Genesee country to the Mohawk Valley, Otetiani found much unrest in 1775. The next year the Indians were approached by both British and Americans to find out what they would do if war should break out. At first, except for the Mohawk, no Iroquois tribe wanted anything to do with an open war. Summing up the feelings of his people, an Oneida chief had told Americans, "We beg of you, take care what you do!"

The determined colonists throughout a wide area, Otetiani learned, felt that they had endured enough and in common with the Boston people were arming for an all-out resistance to British rule.

Samuel Kirkland, in a message from Congress, had been told why the ire of the colonists had been aroused. The Indians insisted that he explain this letter. Kirkland read it to the Oneida chiefs but counseled their neutrality. Sir John Johnson was furious at this and accused the missionary of alienating the loyalty of the now partly Christianized Oneida.

Runners of the Iroquois confederacy were not slow to circulate Kirkland's version of the colonists' complaints, and when the Tuscarora and Stockbridge agreed that the settlers had been wronged, the division of opinion between Kirkland's Oneida converts and the Mohawk grew wider. Still, in spite of promises at the colonists' councils and heaps of presents, the illicit war machine of the Seneca, Cayuga, and Mohawk swung to Joseph Brant. Try as it would, the grand council of sachems could not command neutrality or stay the sentiments of fighting men. Arguments flew back and forth until it appeared that the league had lost all power to act as a unit. The Oneida and Tuscarora wanted to remain neutral friends of the Americans; the rest of the Iroquois wanted to join the British.

By 1777 a leading Oneida declared, "Our council fire is extinguished and can no longer burn." A mixed loyalty could no longer hold together the people of the league for any common action. Then the Mohawk warriors soon came out with an open declaration of allegiance to the British, and the Oneida and their friends openly sided with the Americans. Kirkland's teachings had prevailed, though he had not invited his converts to enter the war.

When there seemed no hope of neutrality, despite promises, Congress had resolved, "that it is highly expedient to engage Indians in the service of the American colonies; and they empower the Commander in Chief to employ, in Canada and elsewhere."

Since the British had enlisted Indians, why did not the Americans? The answer was now direct—the Indians were in the war on both sides.

Whichever way he now looked, the Indian saw himself in the midst of a feud that was bound to leave him the loser whatever the outcome might be. If the white man was divided, so was he. It was now the Seneca and the Mohawk, on the side of the British, against the Oneida and the "bush" nations, who were pro-American. Who would win? Otetiani pondered this question and sought the counsel of Chief Big Tree, known to be a friend of Washington.

In 1775 Joseph Brant had gone to England to represent the Mohawk nation. There he was enthusiastically received by British authorities as an officer of the British army and a commander of the Mohawk. When he returned to his people, therefore, he had been thoroughly impressed with the vast resources of Great Britain. In his opinion Britain could not fail in a contest with feeble and quarreling colonies whatever might be their plea.

Brant's enthusiastic account of Great Britain was also carried by runners to Seneca war councils, and the convictions of these doughty warriors were deepened. They whooped that they were on the winning side at last. The colonists, who had invaded their lands, now would get the punishment that was overdue.

Otetiani heard the arguments of war chiefs and the demands of warrior councils that the colonists must be driven from their homes and pushed back to the lines where treaties had put them. To him, however, the American colonists, whatever might be their sins, were neighbors. He counseled peace and neutrality but heard the sharp accusation he most dreaded, "You are a coward!"

"I am not a coward," he would respond. "Let no man say that; I will defend my nation if its territory is invaded."

"You are like an Oneida; you prefer a soft couch, the cornfields, and the soft voices of the women!" came the taunting snarl of warriors.

"Those who listen to the mothers of the nation and keep the ancient faith know wherein is the life of our people," he would respond. Then he would add, "If we enter this war, our nation will suffer as it never suffered before. Big Tree, Washington's friend, has seen the might of the good men who are our neighbors, and he believes in their triumph. I believe."

"Then you won't fight?"

"I will fight side by side with my people but with sorrow because of their great mistake."

Otetiani thus found himself in the midst of a situation from which he could not extricate himself. The war was on, and he was in it.

The Seneca war machine, now totally separated from the Six Nations council, was under the spell of the masterful Brant. By means of Seneca and Mohawk spies and

British intelligence, the news of every major move of the colonists seeped into the Seneca towns. In the larger villages of Canawaugus, Tonawanda, and Kanadesaga, there were British agents who were encouraging the Seneca to bring supplies to Fort Niagara. Genesee Castle, where Little Beard lived and ruled, was the center of a crop-growing enterprise. The soil there was yielding thousands of bushels of corn, beans, wheat, barley, and many varieties of garden vegetables.

Believed to be inaccessible to colonial troops, its population had grown and its wild fields had expanded to large dimensions. It had 128 well-built houses, "many of them large and elegant," as American officers later described the spot. Its supply bins and storage barns were crammed full even before the autumn harvest. Here lived a busy and contented people, deriving a good income from the British, yet living their own lives as Indians.

It was at Genesee Castle, however, that Indian and Tory leaders were conspiring, matching in importance the centers of the Mohawk people, who had a town at Ouaquaga near the present site of East Windsor. Thus Genesee Castle was believed beyond the reach of Yankee rebels, who were without competent guides.

As Otetiani swiftly ran from council to council to British outposts, he heard the rumor that Brant intended to raid outlying settlements and fortified places in the Unadilla region and on the Susquehanna in Pennsylvania. The most exciting news at this time was that Colonel Barry St. Leger, with seventeen hundred British troops and Indian allies, was planning to attack Fort Schuyler in the Mohawk Valley, a spot not far from the present Utica.

It was to be a battle royal in which the ragged farmers of the valley would be defeated with terrible losses.

"Come just to see us whip the rebels and to watch them run," invited the Tory agents. "You need only sit down and smoke your pipes while we sweep the field."

Otetiani, as an official British messenger, took this message to the waiting settlements of his own people, who received it with much glee. They would sit in an amphitheater and watch the bloody drama! Here was one great chance to witness a fight without the loss of a man and then to loot the supplies that the Yankees would cravenly abandon. As Mary Jemison, the white woman who lived as a captive among the Seneca, wrote in her biography, "The Indians went to a man."

Over the trails they went with their horses and an occasional cart or wagon, carrying with them their ancestral war bundles, charms that ensured victory. Otetiani went along, too, but he took only his pipe.

Expertly officered and splendidly equipped, the British began their march. The colonists under General Nicholas Herkimer knew of their coming, as did Colonel Gansevoort at the fort. Nicholas Herkimer would come to relieve the fort if attacked.

A battle was fought on the fields of Oriskany, "The Place of Nettles." There, for the first time, the Stars and Stripes floated over a battle line. Fort Schuyler was surrounded, and a demand for surrender was made, which was refused with contempt. The sound of distant guns now warned Herkimer that the battle was on, and he marched to the relief of the fort.

It was not long before Herkimer, clumsily moving forward, ran into an ambush and the fighting began. Taken by surprise and not being able to use effectively all their resources, Herkimer's men fought a desperate battle face to face and hand to hand. Herkimer's horse was shot down, and the general was wounded in the leg. Forming a ring, the farmers fought on, their shots telling with deadly accuracy. Then came a drenching rain that made fighting among the trees more difficult than ever. Brave Oneida warriors, rushing in and out of the lines, seemed to be everywhere, giving the news of the British losses and aiding beleaguered flanks. The tide of battle ebbed and flowed, and to the dimming eyes of Herkimer there seemed a lessening of enemy fire. Soon the lines of redcoats began to withdraw and then to move hastily away. Something had happened. The Seneca, seeing their British friends retreat, leaped into the fray but found themselves overcome by the press of the American farmers. Then St. Leger began a retreat toward his base at Oswego.

With persistence and more ardor he might have won the field, for the Yankees were badly hit. But St. Leger knew only that he had been resisted with a fury he had not expected. He abandoned his camp and his supplies and began a wild flight back to the cover of his stronghold on Lake Ontario. His Indian allies began to hoot in derision, and to annoy their fleeing allies further, they began to shout, "News, news, the Americans are coming with a bigger army!"

British soldiers threw away their guns and all excess baggage, fleeing with unconcealed fright. But American troops, far from pursuing, were binding up their wounds and still holding the field and the fort. Who won? The British say they did because of the damage done to Herkimer's raw recruits; the Americans say they did because the British abandoned the field.

And what of the Seneca warriors who came to watch and to smoke their pipes? Thirty-six of their leading men were killed, and many more were wounded; their baggage and their war charms had been lost. It was an unexpected calamity for them, one that seemed to Otetiani to be prophetic of what was to come.

Mary Jemison, who at the time was living at Genesee Castle under Little Beard's protection, told how the Indians there received the news of the defeat. "Our town exhibited a scene of real sorrow and distress," she said, "when our warriors recounted their misfortunes and stated the losses they had sustained in the engagement. The mourning was excessive and was expressed in doleful yells, shrieks and howlings and by inimitable gesticulations."

Such was the ceremonial mourning considered needful to allay the anguish of the dead while treading the sky path. In the religious belief of the Seneca, the souls of the dead are relieved of their suffering, as they are borne into the upper world, by the knowledge that their friends have cared. More than that, it was believed in the old days that, to banish pain along the celestial trail, the suffering of a victim, a prisoner, was necessary unless a captive could be adopted, ceremonially cleansed, and "raised up" to represent each soul. The Seneca thought of this old custom, and some promised to revive it by ravishing border towns and spilling enemy blood.

Soon followed the union of Iroquois forces under Old King and the Tory troops under Butler. A chance came to storm the forts at Wyoming in Pennsylvania. Brant was not there, and in command of Indian warriors, in so far as they could be commanded, was Old King. It is said that no women or children were killed, but it is certain that many of the soldiers were.

Soon, under the command of Joseph Brant, Mohawk and Seneca troops were engaged to fall upon Cherry Valley in New York. Colonel John Butler and his son Walter led the Tory troops that engaged in this battle.

Cherry Valley's safety had been put in the hands of an unwary commander, Colonel Ichabod Alden, whose optimism was so unbounded that he let his officers stay in town, though they were directed to man the fort under his command. He relaxed his vigilance and soothed the villagers into a sense of false security. Then Brant and Butler struck.

Buildings were burned, and the inhabitants were shot or tomahawked, some without mercy. Brant tried to save some women and children by stamping their faces with his seal, but Butler's men showed little mercy to those who rebelled against the British king.

Wyoming and now Cherry Valley! These were scars that reflected little credit upon British policy or upon Iroquois arms, but they roused Americans to the desperate situation that faced them unless Indian power were broken and the Tories were driven out. George Washington felt that he must let border towns recruit their own militia, for on the real front, where the British were pressing the main attack, he needed every man who could be mustered. By the spring of 1779 he had planned a way of handling the marauding Iroquois of western New York. Though the

Indians had undoubted reason to be resentful, they had overstepped and, moreover, had broken an early promise to remain neutral. A dire, merciless punishment must be dealt out. The British-sympathizing Indians must be swept from the face of the earth, or, lacking that, every article of food in the Seneca and Cayuga homelands must be destroyed. Such was Washington's official order to General Gates.

Otetiani now was to have his first real taste of battle and his first experience in a major expedition. He had not taken up arms before, which was his privilege, and his career so far had branded him as a pacifist and even a coward. How could he live that calumny down and at the same time remain true to his belief?

The question that faced Otetiani was whether or not he could come out alive from any struggle with the American settlers. Frontiersmen were seldom poor shots, and each Seneca presented a tantalizing target. It was a predicament that troubled Otetiani, for if the soldiers of Washington did not reach him with bullets, then an irate tribesman might. Well did he know that only those who believed in killing all enemies were wanted in the ranks of war parties. He was not a killer, and to his tribal war chiefs that was bad, bad all around.

As the thunder over the horizon rumbled an omen of a coming storm, Otetiani wondered if, indeed, he would be "Always Ready" in action as well as in name. Time would tell.

[6] *THE TORNADO OF FIRE*

SPRINGTIME ALONG the shining Finger Lakes and in the
deep-loamed valley of the Genesee River never had come
with more promise. Otetiani, as he ran the narrow trails
from Kanadesaga to Niagara, could not fail to see the
myriads of passenger pigeons that flocked in clouds and
covered the sky for miles. These would soon be nesting in
the open woods, and thousands would be taken for food.

As the season advanced, the Indian orchards of peaches,
plums, apples, and pears had richly blossomed. Speeding
across the Genesee flats, Otetiani noted the newly prepared
fields, some of them already springing to life with green

acres of corn, beans, sunflowers, and squashes. The white man's plants, too, were there, and he could see acres of wheat, rye, and oats, some of which had been nibbled by deer.

In their hamlets and larger towns, the Seneca and Cayuga were celebrating their strawberry thanksgiving, and the ominous year of 1779 was one of special joy. Walking through the crowds of young people, Otetiani saw the gleeful youths of Seneca land all exuberant with the sheer love of life. They were playing lacrosse and ground hockey in the village squares, and often he was asked to serve as referee. The young people held him in awe, for he was usually a silent man; but when he spoke, his words had authority. He settled many a dispute when quarrels arose over points in their games. When all was quiet again, he would sit down and view the sport with a faraway look, and sometimes he shook his head as if wondering whether this carefree happiness of young people would long endure.

On one occasion he ran up the river from Canawaugus, where he often stayed, to the great town of Genesee Castle where Little Beard ruled with his frown and his fist. Otetiani noted the British soldiers in their bright uniforms and the officers who were inspecting stables and storehouses. Others were looking over the wheat fields and urging gunsmiths to hasten in their tasks of repairing muskets. Cattle lowed in the meadows, horses galloped across the fields, and swine grunted hopefully as they rooted for grubs and worms. The observing Otetiani saw with an appraising eye that the Western Gate of the Long House of the Iroquois was lush with the scented bloom of a coming harvest and that its meadows supported numerous animals that made hunting less necessary.

With all this for happiness, there was yet a worried look on the faces of the sachems and the women. Warriors scowled as they oiled their muskets and whetted their knives, sometimes feeling the edges and grinning savagely. When Big Tree came over from Honeoye, he would sit in the council lodge. After the village fathers had discussed the preparations for the year, he would stir their fears with his speculations about the movements of the Americans. "They are angry about Cherry Valley and Wyoming," he would testify. "Be sure they are not going to remain idle. I know the spirit of Washington, and I know that he is very angry because we have not kept the promise of some of our chiefs to be neutral."

"What about the white settlers?" a war chief would ask. "Are they to be ignored when they attack us?"

Otetiani sat with deep concern as he listened to these councils in which the affairs of his nation were discussed. Big Tree was one of his friends, and he had followed him from one village to another. Big Tree's warning was always the same, "Beware of war with a determined people."

"What would you have us now do?" a sachem would ask.

"We should be friendly with our white neighbors," he would say. "Not all are the rogues you think they are. That man Washington is a leader to watch, and I am glad to say that I am his friend."

"Washington's friend?" would come the retort. "You'll be sorry when he sends soldiers to shoot you. Our real friends, the British, say he is a rebel, a deserter from his king's army, a hater of Indians."

"Washington is just and merciful, I know. Once he gave me a blanket when I was cold."

"But the British say he is just waiting for a chance to drive us into the western wilderness and that he may invade our country."

"If invaded, I will fight those who come," replied Big Tree. "My friend would expect that, and you may count on it. But I'd rather we were at peace with my friend and his people."

"Humph, you are like Otetiani, who listens to women and old men. He has no more spirit than you, Big Tree and little heart," an arrogant warrior would sneer. "Don't you know that no army can reach us? Don't you know that only our fringes will be torn? Here we are safe, and from here we can swoop down and take our revenge."

How lacking in foresight these unlettered men of the wilderness were! They had listened to rumors many times before, and nothing had happened; life continued as usual. It just couldn't happen!

The real facts they did not know. They did not know that the frontier had suffered enough from depredation and from the determination of the Indians to make treaties stick. They did not know how sorely the colonists were tired of British rule. They did not understand that, right or wrong, the colonists' temptation to take the land that spread before them was stronger than law or religion, treaties or prayers. They did not know that the race-will of Englishmen, tinctured with the spirit of Vikings and bolstered by the belief that "the Lord God of Israel had destined them to take the land of the Philistines," was a deep will and would not be denied. They did not know many other things, nor could they have understood some of them if they had been told.

One practical fact, however, they might have understood had they known of it in time. It was that in the hands of a New Hampshire lawyer who had become a general in the American army was a letter from General George Washington, who had written, "It is proposed to carry the war into the heart of the country of the Six Nations, to cut off their settlements, destroy their next year's crops, and do them every other mischief which time and circumstances will permit."

To this lawyer, whose name was John Sullivan, Washington repeated his instructions, "The immediate objects are the total destruction of the hostile tribes of the Six Nations, and the devastation of their settlements, and the capture of as many prisoners of every age and sex as possible."

Washington knew that he was taking a great risk. If Sullivan met defeat, the Indians would bathe the frontier in blood. It was only his faith in an ultimate triumph of arms that lent him courage to carry out his plan. Of this determination the British soon became keenly aware, and they quickly passed the threat along to the Indians. The information was carried by Otetiani from one settlement to another, and secondary runners sped the news that a vast army was forming down the Susquehanna. There had been rumors before that had come to nothing. Life went on as usual, only a few wiser people making preparations for what might happen.

During the late summer, shouts were heard along the trails, and village sentinels noted that couriers from Brant's headquarters came speeding into the town squares with the death cry, "*Goweh! goweh! goweh!*" It was the signal of coming disaster.

"From the Susquehanna flats they are coming, coming like grasshoppers, many soldiers, many cannons. We are ordered by Brant to hasten to a rendezvous at Chemung." Such was the burden of the warning.

At hastily convened councils the urgency of the situation was placed before the people. The sachems and the women covered their eyes to hide their tears, for they knew that invasion would mean the loss of many of their people and possibly the loss of the land. Yet all knew that, if soldiers came, there must be resistance. If any failed to realize this, the agents of Brant and Butler made the fact understood.

Somewhere and at some time Otetiani had taken a wife whom some called Wyashoh, the talkative one, and there were children. Otetiani's first reaction was to find a place of refuge for his family before he joined his fellow warriors to meet the enemy. No one knows just where the hiding place was, but later generations of Indians have speculated that it was either at a spot just east of Canandaigua or on Squaw Island in Canandaigua Lake. He was to rejoin his family if there was a retreat.

Within a few hours after Brant's command had been given, the trails toward Chemung were alive with hundreds of warriors, each laden with battle equipment. The men had food, spare clothing, moccasins, medicines, and ammunition. Some carried ornamental ropes and beautifully decorated prisoner ties, embroidered with moose or elk-beard hair or with porcupine quills. There were war paint and small tools for the repair of guns and clothing. Some Indians carried magical charms that they believed would protect them from bullets, and some carried charmed medicine that cured wounds almost instantly.

So burdened, a long line of softly treading moccasined feet sped through the forest. Like the rest Otetiani slept on the ground, greased his face to repel flies and mosquitoes, mixed water with his pemmican meal, and ate the green herbs that grew abundantly.

Once again on the march, he would note with mixed feelings the presence of mounted Rangers from Butler's forces or fast-speeding messengers from Johnson's Royal Greens. There was but one message, "Speed up, speed up!" Otetiani as tribal runner hastened to relay the order, often returning to confer with the aged Old King who was nominally in charge of the Seneca warriors.

At length about a thousand Indians and half that number of British soldiers assembled near Chemung for a planned attack on the avenging enemy, now reported by spies to be near at hand. Otetiani heard his commander say that an ambush and surprise attack might turn the foe back with terrible losses. But could the fifteen hundred frighten the thousands that Brant's spies had reported in the opposing army? Otetiani did not believe it possible.

He soon learned the strategy that Captain Brant had planned. It was not immediately to ambush the oncoming army of General Sullivan. Instead the American army was to be allowed a little success as encouragement. It would then be lured to a location farther north near the settlement called Newtown. This plan had been in Brant's mind since the previous summer, when he had suspected

Sullivan's strategy, the tactics that now were actually in operation. Thus he set his sun-tanned warriors at work throwing up breastworks and a screen of evergreen trees at a point between the Chemung River and a long, finger-like hill to the east.

The story of the expedition of Sullivan and Clinton is an exciting one, and their march toward a planned meeting at Tioga Point, or at some point westward along the river, was a masterly military accomplishment. Its details later even excited the admiration of the Seneca, who were never slow to give the enemy credit.

The two American armies did meet as planned, and the occasion was one for shouts and the sound of martial music. The spies of Brant and Butler heard the triumphant shout which told them that Clinton had broken through. They heard also the more alarming threat of the salute of thirteen rounds of artillery. Then there were more shouts, band music, the roll of drums, and loud cheers. The Indians could endure the cheers, but the voice of the cannon disturbed them greatly.

Otetiani and his fellow scouts, hidden in the forest, heard the cannon's boom, heard the triumphant shouts, and then sped up the Chemung to tell an amazing story of invaders without number and of a gun whose report rivaled that of the Thunder God.

"Let us here make peace before we are totally destroyed!" argued Otetiani. "War like this can only strip away all our possessions and take our lives." He resolved to test the will of Sullivan at the very first chance, not knowing how futile it would be.

With amazement and fear, the next morning the Indian

rear guard heard a cannon boom and saw an army start out on its march. At its rear were horses and cattle and toiling men burdened with baggage and supplies. Horses were plunging, stumbling, and almost groaning under their loads, while men with whips were urging them on.

Eagerly waiting to see how this formidable force might be met, Otetiani with the privilege of a runner sought the British headquarters and found that Colonel John Butler and his officers were relying on Brant's ability to arrange a trap into which the Americans could be lured and shot down. Though there was some scattered shooting by the Indians, this did not stop the American soldiers from slashing at the growing corn with their sabers and starting fires at the abandoned Seneca outpost at Chemung.

The destruction of food plants was a sin in the minds of the Seneca, who regarded the life of plants as sacred. They could understand that men might fight men, but it seemed wrong for men to fight corn and trees. But the burning went on, and Otetiani knew that it would continue as long as the great army remained unchecked.

But now there was a trap. The hope ran high that, before another town was reached, the enemy might be checked. It was a case of the waiting fifteen hundred British and Indians against nearly three times that number of confident Americans, many of whom knew the way of the woods. Yet it was hoped that the ambush and the breastworks might furnish a shield that would make a base for effective resistance—if only the Americans were not so numerous.

The woodwise eyes of General Sullivan's advance party quickly detected the concealed fortification. Cannons were brought up, and havoc began as the balls splintered trees and crashed through branches. Again and again the Tory and Indian defenders poured volleys of musketry in the direction of their foe but with little effect. The cannons still boomed out with devastating results. Driven from their shelter, the Indians and their allies took to the hill to their left and rear, but this move had been anticipated. From both flanks, front and rear, Sullivan's brigades made their attack, the defenders slowly backing northward.

Again and again, amid a rain of bullets, Brant sought to rally his frightened troops, now demoralized and nearly exhausted; but nothing could withstand the American soldiery, well equipped and in favorable numbers. Cannons placed on an elevation raked the Tory-Indian front. Troops were encircling them, and men were falling in alarming numbers. For Brant and Butler there was now but one thing to do—retreat.

In the face of this necessity, according to Brant's testimony, Otetiani detailed two of his command to take a message to Sullivan offering to cease fire if an armistice were granted. Brant discovered the gesture and had the two messengers shot. Whether this is an accurate statement, we do not know, but it does reveal Brant's early animosity toward the Seneca leader of the peace movement. Brant again was to sneer at Otetiani's cowardice as the retreat progressed.

So rapidly did the Tory battalions and Indian troops scatter that they overlooked other strategic points along the way where it would have been easy for an ambush of a thousand men to do terrible damage to the floundering American troops as they wallowed through a cedar swamp.

The chance was missed at the very point where it would have delayed the expedition and assisted in other efforts to harass it. Not until the hills of Conesius had been reached, was there another encounter worthy of note.

Thus Sullivan and his four thousand followed the well-beaten trail, slowly driving the cattle and horses, but reached town after town only to find and burn empty dwellings. With this work of the torch came the task of slashing down hundreds of acres of corn and other growing crops. The corn was in its August prime, perfect for boiling or roasting. So rapidly did the army march that in several places the soldiers found succotash, sweet corn, fresh beans, and other foods boiling in pots that had been abandoned but a few minutes before. Great orchards, some with fifteen hundred trees, were hacked down or girdled. The order not to allow one morsel of food to remain for the Indians who might return had been explicit. The great, billowing columns of smoke which Otetiani saw rolling skyward confirmed his worst fears.

In this manner village after village perished. Plantation after plantation and orchard after orchard were attacked with ax, saber, and torch. Onward went the work of flame and spade until the Americans reached Kanadesaga on September 7. Here were sixty large houses, some smaller ones, a half-ruined blockhouse, large fields of growing crops, orchards, and gardens. Not an enemy could be found; there was only a half-starved white child, whom the soldiers took along with them. Two days later the castle of Old King was burned to ashes, together with its fields and storehouses. The "grand village" of the eastern Seneca had fallen, and with the last wisp of smoke Wyoming had been revenged. But when his capital town perished, Old King was not to know it. He had fallen at the Battle of Newtown, if we are to believe the reports of the invading army.

As the Tories and Indians raced against time and pursuit, Brant became sternly aware of the panic flight of his forces, now hampered by hundreds of fleeing women and children. Numerous warriors had found members of their families and had attempted to lead them to safety. But there also were hundreds of lost children, tired old women, and crippled old men, some of whom were bent under the burden of a few possessions which they treasured.

With all this before him, Brant could not resist the challenge to make one more effort to strike at the foe. He advised his diminished forces to make a stand near the foot of Canandaigua Lake, probably at the point where the present Bristol Street meets Thad Chapin Road. A boulder with a bronze marker locates the spot. Here he advised Otetiani of his intention and ordered the Seneca warriors to halt and form an ambush.

"We stand here and fight," Brant commanded.

"I will not consent to any such action," retorted Otetiani.

"Coward, coward!" yelled Brant.

"You have said that before," replied Otetiani. "Nevertheless, I shall not sacrifice my men or the safety of these women, children, and old people who need our aid in escaping."

Brant looked at Otetiani's wife, who had rejoined him, and said with bitter sarcasm, "Leave that man; leave him, lest your children have a coward for a father!"

The irate and frustrated Mohawk chief might have made a stand himself, but even with the aid of British troops and his own warriors, he thought better of it and continued his retreat. On and on the Indians hurried, heading for Genesee Castle and Canawaugus. Once there, the women and children could escape to Fort Niagara, and the men could make a stand at the castle where Little Beard held forth.

Sullivan by this time was painfully aware of his shortage of supplies, and though he had expected to drive through to Fort Niagara, this now seemed a remote possibility. He was far from his base at Fort Sullivan, where he had left two hundred men with the six-pounders, and his cows and horses were thin and weak because of the difficulties of travel.

After leaving Canandaigua, he burned the settlements through which he passed and pressed toward the valley, where he supposed that on the east side of the river lay Genesee Castle. He did not know that the town had been moved across the river and three miles upstream.

Arriving at Honeoye, a small village of twenty houses, Sullivan left the lame and the lazy and a force of fifty men, who fortified themselves in a log house, stacking the bags of flour against the timbers like sandbags. From this point the army marched on to Conesius, a village of eighteen houses, where Captain Sun Fish, a Negro, lived and made himself useful to the villagers. Big Tree lived here also, and when his settlement was burned, his associates with sarcasm asked what he thought of his "friends" now. To this he replied that, because he was in bad company, his friends could not distinguish what was his and what was their enemy's.

From their hiding place in a bushy growth, the Indians saw the army march out toward Conesius. By this time

Otetiani, lingering at Big Tree's side, knew that the enemy would find the town of Genesee Castle, where the forces of Brant and his Tory friends were attempting to muster their forces for one last stand before Sullivan marched to Fort Niagara. At once Otetiani gathered his little family and fled northward to Canawaugus and from there hurried on to Tonawanda village and Niagara.

Seneca scouts saw the march proceed and saw the ambush and capture of Sullivan's advance party. The victorious army which Washington had sent was seen crossing the river and entering Genesee Castle.

Genesee Castle was the most western objective which Sullivan reached. His supplies were low, and from here he turned back to seek out the towns along the two larger lakes. Otetiani's natal village near Cayuga Lake was put to the torch when a detachment reached it in September. In all, forty Indian settlements had been reduced to ashes with the loss of only a few men.

Some important places like Canawaugus and Caneadea were not touched, and the more westerly settlements on the Tonawanda were overlooked because they were not known to the Oneida guides. These villages were crowded with refugees, who soon found it a wiser plan to press forward to Niagara where British guns would protect them and military stores would provide food. Otetiani and his family went to Niagara where there was work for a courier, even a grieving one.

He had seen the almost total destruction of the land he loved and the implements and tribal treasures perish in flames. It is related that he never smiled again. Though more than a thousand of his fellow warriors and almost all the women and children had escaped, starvation faced them since so large a number of refugees certainly would tax the ability of the Niagara commissary to provide food for all. There was only one circumstance to cause satisfaction, and that was the extraordinary flight of the women and children. Often they were only a few minutes ahead of the pursuing army, but there is no record that any were captured. After the destruction of Genesee Castle there were no more pursuits, though for a full century the elders of families descended from Indian warriors told of their ancestors being hunted in the woods by American soldiers.

The success of the expedition of destruction was without a flaw, and in a military sense Otetiani saw that it was a remarkable achievement. It was carried out with great boldness but with a military force more than equal to the total population that it sought to upset. It was many years before the Indians learned of Sullivan's address of congratulation to his troops as they turned back toward Tioga. He said, "The Commander in Chief informs this brave and resolute army that the immediate object of this expedition has been accomplished; namely, total destruction of the Indian settlements and the destruction of their crops, which were designed for the support of these inhuman barbarians while they were devastating the American frontiers."

Otetiani had survived bullets and now he survived starvation, obtaining fuller supplies for his family because of his services as an army runner. His tattered raiment now was replaced by a British military coat of red with epaulets of gilt upon the shoulders. This conspicuous dress, coupled with his better fed appearance in a starving camp, made him the subject of much unfavorable comment. Nor was

his popularity among the warriors enhanced by his smugness or his "I told you so!" His unhappy tribesmen did not
like to be reminded that he had disapproved of their course
and had frowned upon their bloody deeds.

As many warriors said then and in later years, "Otetiani is just too smart for his buckskins." But the sad truth,
they knew, was that he was right. Otetiani, the always
ready, had the misfortune of being always right. This hurt
those who were often wrong.

[7] *THE WHIRLWIND SUBSIDES*

WHEN SPRINGTIME CAME to Niagara in 1780, the lean and scurvy-tortured Indians, grubbing in the woods for roots or seeking new hemlock shoots and other greens, began to stir themselves again. The war on the western front had subsided, and Sullivan's town destroyers had gone home.

Well did the hungry Seneca and Cayuga tribesmen know that towns could be rebuilt and that ash-strewn land would grow new crops from seed that Canawaugus and Tonawanda might supply. Until new crops could be grown, however, the returning refugees had to find food in the ground itself. There were many roots, such as those of artichokes, pond lilies, and groundnuts, that could be gathered. Women gathered the shoots of raspberry stalks, green twigs, and the inner core of the cattail or its slimy root, and some peeled the inner bark of the slippery elm—all good emergency food. The men hunted for raccoon, rabbit, bear, and deer, but a larger supply of flesh came from the brooks and ponds where fish were easily caught.

At first the new lodges were small and individual. It took strength to build the great long houses again, but it was not long before clusters of shacks began to appear on the sites of once more prosperous-looking towns. New utensils, tools, and weapons were made, and there was even time to carve out new ceremonial objects like feast bowls and masks, or false faces.

It was at Niagara that Otetiani had become known as Red Jacket, having been given, as we have seen, a coat of military red ornamented with gilt braid. This was an easier name for the British, who had so often used his fleetness on the trail to their advantage when dispatches were to be sent. His red jacket, with a white shirt beneath, and his blue leggings neatly decorated with beads made him a conspicuous figure. It is believed that he enjoyed being an object of interest, having a streak of vanity not entirely unknown to the British officers whom he served as a courier.

With his red coat and his well-fitted clothing he had attained a new individuality, and when he addressed either a council of his own people or a gathering of officers at the fort, he was now pointed out as Red Jacket. His conspicuous position as an official messenger and his eloquent speeches before tribal meetings brought him another honor. He was now deemed worthy of a new Seneca name, and

the tribal elders selected and bestowed the name title
Sagoyewatha, meaning "He keeps them awake."

In his more elevated station Red Jacket continued to address his people, cautioning them to serve their own interests first before they lost everything in serving others.
A dead nation, he insisted, is of no value to the world. But
whom now could the disillusioned Seneca trust; could they
even trust themselves?

The hope of the broken Indian nations was still with the
British who, even after the treaty of peace, held Niagara,
Oswego, Detroit, and other posts along the Great Lakes.
British military officers continued to provide food, clothing, arms, and tools to their red allies and regarded them
as their special wards, well knowing the apparent hostility
of the victorious Americans.

If the westernmost of the Six Nations would not abandon their old territory, the eastern groups would. This was
especially true of the Mohawk. Under Joseph Brant they
had accepted a grant of land in Canada, six miles wide on
either side of the Grand River, extending from mouth to
source. This was to be the promised haven and reward for
the loss of their New York holdings. A new adventure and
a new hope were to be found in this old land of the destroyed Neutral Nation, a portion of which the Seneca had
absorbed after 1650. This wide and fertile tract had been
awarded in the name of the king by Sir Frederick Haldi-
mand, a crown officer in Canada. To this pleasant location
all members of the Six Nations and their dependents had
been invited, and representatives of all had accepted,
dividing the population left in New York. They still con-

sidered themselves one people, separated only by the fact that some had chosen new villages.

Notwithstanding this bright promise of a new freedom, many Iroquois preferred their old homeland. For a long time after the war little villages of Seneca, Cayuga, Mohawk, and Tuscarora were dotted along the Niagara from Youngstown to Fort Schlosser. The mighty cataract and the wide river ever had fascinated Red Jacket. He often stood at Table Rock when the full moon rode the sky, gazing at the tumbling thunder waters and waiting for the lunar rainbow. The British encouraged these lingering red men to seek another location, and the Americans felt that this was wise. Thus a new tract of land was cleared along Buffalo Creek, and gradually all the Niagara refugees moved away from the fort, relieving the British of the problem of feeding them. It was not long before eight busy little hamlets with their gardens and fields appeared along another stream where older nations had lived, for Buffalo Creek had many evidences of the presence of a once energetic people.

Red Jacket did not immediately leave Niagara for Buffalo because Niagara was a place where he could mingle with the soldiers of the fort. There he could meet important chiefs and receive an occasional commission as a messenger and dispatch carrier. To Niagara often came Farmer's Brother, the aging veteran of the Devil's Hole affair, Half Town, Young King, Cornplanter, Little Billy, Kenjockety, Clear Sky, and Pollard. There, too, were likable British Indians like Captain David and Captain Aaron Hill, both of whom were English-speaking Mohawk officers.

Among all these only Red Jacket and Farmer's Brother

stood out as forceful orators. Each had a command of words that at once attracted attention. When the Revolution ended, it was Farmer's Brother who said, "The Great Spirit spoke to the whirlwind and it was still."

As a runner for both Indians and whites, Red Jacket heard many rumors that had filtered through the forest over the tongues of Tory agitators or from the mouths of overzealous Yorkers. He heard how the New York legislature was about to dispossess their old friends and supporters, the Oneida, and force them to occupy Seneca territory. The Oneida people, it was related, were to be fooled by soft words, and then their lands were to be wrested from them by subtle trickery. More than this, all Indians who had aided the British were to be driven out of the state. Later such an expulsion was decided against because a strong body of resentful Indians might do frightful harm to the whites.

One alarming circumstance troubled Red Jacket and disturbed all responsible chiefs; when the treaty of peace between Britain and America was signed, there was not a single word about how the Six Nations should be treated. So far as the United States was concerned, these Indians were still at war with them. Only the Oneida and Tuscarora had any assurance that they would not be expelled, but there were plots even against them. Somehow Britain had left its erstwhile Indian allies to the mercy of the United States. The Seneca, Cayuga, and Onondaga tribes found themselves in the position of being enemies of the United States while living within its borders. They would be subject to reprisal without any protection from their former English sponsors now based in Canada.

President Washington knew the misery that would accompany a new war on the frontier, and so did General Philip Schuyler. It was, therefore, deemed cheaper to arrange a treaty with the Indians assuring them peace in exchange for the surrender of more land than had been specified by the treaty of 1768. Then the Six Nations might stay until bought out later.

In spite of New York's treaty plans, the federal government in 1784 called a treaty council at Fort Stanwix. To it were invited representatives of the Six Nations. The Seneca learned that Cornplanter, now a war captain of their tribe, and a scattering of others had agreed to attend the council. None of them had received instructions from the Indian people. Red Jacket remained aloof, not caring to face the humiliation that would be heaped upon his disorganized and distracted people. Despite later reports to the contrary, he did not attend the council at Fort Stanwix.

At the treaty council Cornplanter was asked to lay out a new boundary line to show what land would now be surrendered. When he hesitated, the American treaty commissioners drew their own line and lectured the Seneca and Cayuga upon their perfidy in aiding the British. Yet, if the Indians would sign this new treaty, all would be forgiven. When there were further discussion and complaint on the part of the Indians, the commissioners recited the power of the United States and its right to compensation for the injuries inflicted by the Indians during the war. "Our words are strong, and we mean that you should feel them," declared General Richard Butler, one of the Americans.

The beleaguered Indians received the strong words like

bullets in their breasts. Urged on by Cornplanter, however, the warriors present signed the treaty with much reluctance, for they had little authority to do so.

Pressure for this treaty and the relinquishment of land was convincingly strong, for the Indians faced not only top military men but such eminent figures as Lafayette, James Madison, and James Monroe. Of the Indians, Captain Aaron Hill seems to have been the most distinguished and able, though others like Cornplanter were there. Hill's speeches pleased his tribesmen, who felt that he was indeed expressing their inner feelings.

"We are free and independent," he declared, "and at present under no influence. We have hitherto been bound to the great king. But because he has broken the chain and left us to ourselves, we are again free and independent."

"You are mistaken," replied General Butler, "mistaken in supposing that you are a free and independent nation and may make what terms you please. It is not so. You are a subdued people; you have been overcome in a war which you entered against us, not only without provocation, but in violation of most sacred obligations."

With these drastic words to sting them, the Indians departed to spread the word of the difference in view between the victory-conscious new nation and the still defiant tribesmen. They were quick to realize that the coup had been aided by the easy capitulation of Cornplanter.

By this treaty they were now committed to the restoration of all white prisoners living with them, and Captain Hill and several other hostages were held by the Americans until such prisoners had been delivered. Some of the prisoners refused to return, and some who did immediately went back to their Indian friends. Mary Jemison for one, having lived so long as a Seneca, did not wish to run the risk of living again with her own race and taking her half-blood brood with her. She thought the wrench would be more than she could endure.

To all Indians the terms of the treaty seemed harsh and the attitude of the commissioners arrogant. Red Jacket was not slow to blame Cornplanter for weakly seeking his own interests at the expense of his people, and this intensified Cornplanter's enmity for his critic. The two never forgave each other.

One of the measures of strategy was for the Indians, aided by British officers, to create a widely distributed confederacy of tribes west of the Ohio, bringing all Indian nations into it. The Six Nations would be placed at the head of this new power. British authorities liked the plan, for if accomplished, it would create a buffer state between Canada and the United States. Joseph Brant was active in furthering the scheme.

At a meeting of trans-Ohio tribesmen two years after the Fort Stanwix treaty, Red Jacket was spokesman for the New York Indian nations. He electrified his hearers by saying, "Though Great Britain has withdrawn from the contest, Indians as original owners of the land ought to make common cause and carry on the contest until the Americans will agree to recognize their rights."

In a similar speech Cornplanter, after having heard the murmuring voices of the eastern Seneca, declared that the Six Nations had agreed to the American demands at Fort Stanwix only because of threats. "You then told us that we were in your hand," he stated, "and that by closing it you could crush us to nothing, and you demanded from us a great country as the price of the peace you had offered us—as though our want of strength had destroyed our rights."

Plainly there was a division of opinion between the government of the United States and the Six Nations. Neither party understood the principles which governed the other's thinking. Each excused itself and blamed the other.

[8] *FLINT AND STEEL*
ON THE BORDER

AFTER THE AMERICAN REVOLUTION, Red Jacket was astonished to learn that the land of his ancestors no longer
belonged to the Seneca nation. A British king long ago had
given the title of the soil to the Massachusetts Bay colony,
and the colony had now become a state. New York wanted
to extend its laws over its territory, and Massachusetts
agreed to yield its sovereignty but insisted on retaining
its right to sell the land to a convenient buyer.

Here was a chance for someone to make a great profit.
Two Massachusetts men, named Nathaniel Gorham and

Oliver Phelps, seized the opportunity. They offered Massachusetts a million dollars for the part of western New York that reaches from Seneca Lake to the Genesee River. They realized that the Indians had a right of occupancy. However, they felt that this right could be bought.

Accordingly, they offered the Seneca nation a paltry $5,000 for the land and agreed to give $500 to the Seneca each year forever. By making many promises, including an agreement that the "graves of Indians shall never be disturbed," they were able to persuade the Indians to sign an agreement. Red Jacket had argued against such a sale, but when other chiefs consented, he reluctantly bowed to the will of the majority and agreed to the transfer of the land to the white men.

Though the land in question was only thinly settled by Indians, the red men still liked to feel that they controlled a vast territory. The Phelps-Gorham sale stripped them of many hundreds of thousands of acres, and this gave rise to much dissatisfaction.

Because of sharp dealing like this, many younger Indians who had no part in the councils became angry. Tribes beyond the Ohio also had "sold" their land, either because of threats or because of the use of actual force. They, too, were alarmed at the results. This loss of territory made many wandering bands along the Allegheny and Ohio rivers bitter and hostile. In 1790 a bloody conflict was raging in western Pennsylvania and in Virginia. British officers were encouraging resistance by the Indians to further American encroachment. The object of British interference, of course, was to force the American government to concede that the western boundary between the

Americans and the Indians must be placed at the Ohio
River.

The Seneca were quite sympathetic to this scheme to
limit American expansion and looked with a degree of
favor upon the midwestern tribes who fought invasion.
American diplomacy held the Seneca back, however, until
bordermen wantonly murdered two inoffensive young
Seneca trappers.

The Seneca at once were aroused, but the United States
disavowed the act and promised to punish the offenders,
offering a reward for their arrest. It does not appear that
they were ever hanged. Discontent and suspicion deepened, and the younger warriors slipped away to join hostile
tribes and find satisfaction in swooping down on settlers.

It was at this juncture that Colonel Timothy Pickering
was commissioned to call a council at Tioga Point and to
seek to allay the threat of reprisals. Important Seneca
leaders came, among them Red Jacket, Farmer's Brother,
Little Billy, and Fish Carrier, the Cayuga chief. Even Old
Hendrick, the Stockbridge leader who had fought for the
patriots at White Plains, was there.

Pickering came primed for doing things in the ceremonial way of the red men. Yes, he was sorry that their
relatives had been victims of pot shots, and so in ceremonial
manner he "dried their tears and wiped away the blood
that had been shed."

Red Jacket listened politely, and just when all seemed
to be getting off to a good start, he suddenly brought up
the subject of whether or not the Indians had understood
their former sale. "They didn't get all their money," he
declared. This was a pot shot to put Colonel Pickering

on the defensive, and Pickering with a show of anger contradicted the chief. It is quite possible that Red Jacket was right since there is no record of what actually was promised. Some of the oral promises were never included in the written contracts.

The money had been accepted from Phelps and Gorham, and even Red Jacket, after bucking the idea, had signed near the top of the document, perhaps fully believing that by this act he made the sale unanimous. But still he complained.

"We took your money and shared it," he affirmed. "Yes, and when we looked at what we had in our fingers, it was only a dollar apiece."

Little was accomplished at Tioga, and somewhat later another talk was held at Painted Post, a favorite meeting place. Something was wrong, however, and it was hard for American commissioners versed in the law and customs of European civilization to understand the underlying causes of unrest. Some of these causes have been pointed out. However, it may be well to repeat them, just as Red Jacket did at this council, though neither party was able to put the difficulty into formal words.

The trouble was this: The peoples of two diverse cultures, basing their reactions upon old beliefs which each had inherited, quite naturally could not agree. The beliefs of the Indians were not the beliefs of Europeans. Indians never heard of the way Europeans had developed their thinking or how the people of Palestine, Greece, Rome, and England had evolved the rules of their game of civilization.

For example, how could Indians know anything about

the divine right of kings or admit that the mere sight of land from the sea by a sailor or soldier transferred the ownership of the land to the king whose subject saw it? The "poor heathen" had no idea that "discovery" gives a title to the land without regard to the original owners. If a Seneca went over to London, and some did in 1710, he could not conceive that this "discovery" gave him England. If he happened to see the shores of France, he would not claim ownership of Europe. Yet both law and religion were deemed to sustain the belief that "discovery" gave America to its European "discoverers." It was as if the Indians were considered wild animals. Red Jacket saw through this strange notion, and he didn't like it. He wasn't slow in telling every council to which Europeans came that he was against their propositions. He said so at Painted Post and later urged his people to sign no more treaties with whites.

President Washington had more patience than most other men of his time and seemed to see what the trouble was. He thought that, if the Indians could be educated even a little to understand what the white man knew, a great forward movement would be made and all would benefit. He wanted missionaries and teachers to instruct the various tribes about European ways in the hope that both parties would then think alike.

With some such thought in mind, and to remove the suspicions of the Six Nations, Washington invited the leading chiefs of the Seneca and their associates to hold a council with Secretary of War Knox, Colonel Pickering, and himself in Philadelphia. He wanted to overcome the disturbing effect of American military defeats by the western tribes.

After a strenuous journey, fifty chiefs, including Red Jacket and Farmer's Brother, with the Reverend Samuel Kirkland as interpreter and counsel, reached the nation's capital. Washington's views were well known to both federal officials, and they wanted to urge the Indians to follow the Great White Father's advice. Briefly, this was to give up their hunting and fishing, their trapping, and their distant trading for the arts of civilized man. They did not seem to realize that it had been civilized man's quest for vast quantities of furs that had upset the former agricultural economy of the Indians.

"The President advises you to live more like the white people about you," General Knox told his forest friends. "To be more happy and contented, you must follow the plow instead of the deer and then seek the blessings of peace and forsake war."

To this the Indians could only nod their heads and say, "Huh!"

This seemed to satisfy the officials, and the Seneca there were given great hospitality, offered food and drink, and shown the sights of the town and the majesty of its buildings. Thomas Mifflin, Governor of Pennsylvania, then addressed them, hoping they had been greatly stimulated by what they had seen. He told them he wanted them to know how well the Americans welcomed strangers and that he realized fully that the Indians did likewise when strangers came to them.

"It is my sincere wish," said the governor, "that, when

you return to your families, you may be able to assure them that the virtues of friendship and hospitality are also practiced by the citizens of Pennsylvania."

Red Jacket replied in the same happy vein. In part he said, "Though we have no writings like you, yet we remember often to have heard of the friendship that existed between our fathers and yours."

Here he pointed to the painting of William Penn sealing his treaty with the Indians. "The picture to which you drew our attention," Red Jacket went on to say, "brought freshly to our minds the friendly disposition of our people. It is still our wish as well as yours to preserve peace between our tribe and you."

Washington's address was in the same friendly spirit. He wanted peace that should be founded upon the principles of justice and humanity, "as upon an immovable rock." Then the President added:

But in order that our peace and friendship may forever be unclouded, we must forget the misunderstandings of past times. I am aware that existing hostilities of some western Indians have been ascribed to an unjust possession of their lands by the United States. But be assured this is not the case. We require no lands but those obtained by treaties. . . . If the western Indians should entertain the opinion that we want to wrest their lands from them, they are laboring under error.

Just how the Indians took this statement is not known, but it is quite likely that they did not believe. They must have looked at each other and wondered whether or not it could possibly be true that the settlers who were jumping treaty lines did not want more land than the treaties arranged for.

In reply Red Jacket made an impressive speech. For one thing, the Seneca orator said that the lack of certainty among the Indians was caused by a lack of understanding between the Americans and the British; the latter were still holding forts in the western parts of the United States. If there were any question why the Indians were wavering between the British and the United States, it was because of the persistence of the British hold on the frontier.

Then, looking over his audience of leading statesmen, Red Jacket said:

All is in a measure now quieted. Peace is now budding. But still there is some shaking among the original Americans toward the setting sun; and you of the thirteen fires and the king of England know what our situation is and the causes of this disturbance. Now you have an ambassador here, Mr. Hammond, British envoy, as we are informed, from the king of England. Let him, in behalf of his king, and the Americans adjust their differences according to their treaty, and then you will soon see all things settled among the Indian nations. When you Americans and the king made peace, he did not mention us and showed us no compassion, notwithstanding all he said to us and all we had suffered. This has been the occasion of great sorrow and pain and great loss to us. . . . When you and he settled the peace between you, the great nations, he never asked us for a delegation to attend to our interests. Had he done this, a settlement of peace among the western nations might have been effected. But neglect of this has brought upon us great pain and trouble. . . . Our chain of peace has been broken.

In these words Red Jacket explained why the tribes of the Northwest had warred with the Americans and remained uncertain as to whom their allegiance was due and why the Indians were incensed at neglect. The blame was put squarely on the British.

"But you Americans," said Red Jacket, "were determined not to treat us in the same manner as we had been treated by the king of England. You desired us at the re-establishment of peace to sit down at our ancient fire-places and again enjoy our lands. And had the peace between you and the king been completely accomplished, it would long before this have extended to us."

Turning to Colonel Pickering, the orator commented on the hostility of the Miami, Pottawatomie, Shawnee, and other tribes of the Great Lakes and asked him to point out to the Six Nations what he thought the real cause might be. Well did all concerned know that the very fact that the Americans allowed the British to hold forts within American territory was an admission that the British still had authority. These same British were convinced that their authority extended over the Indian tribes who before the Revolution had been enemies of the American settlers. Quite naturally the defeated British were not too cordial to American claims arising from Washington's victory at Yorktown; they still believed that the American states could be discomfited by having enemy Indians west of them. Should the Canadians then find cause for renewal of the war, the Indians as a buffer state would bear the first brunt of the shock. Red Jacket understood that this was the situation and concluded his formal address by showing exactly how to bring the hostilities to direct terms.

"You and the king of England," he said, "are the two governing powers of this island [continent]. What are we? You both are important and proud—and [yet] you cannot adjust your own affairs agreeably to your declarations of peace! Therefore, the western Indians are bewildered. To them one says one thing, and one says another. Were all these things adjusted, it would be easy to bring about peace everywhere."

Red Jacket had put his finger on the very cause of restlessness and of border warfare that had cost the lives of numerous Americans. A hesitating, pussyfooting policy, due to the weakness of the government and the difficulty of raising troops, had been costly in blood and in treasure. Thus the Indians, not knowing which master to serve, served themselves as their advantage lay.

Colonel Pickering had listened with absorbed interest to Red Jacket's analysis and then gave the American side of the picture, pointing out the present friendship of the Six Nations although once they had been enemies. "Perhaps as friends of both sides," he suggested, "you may be willing to speak to the western Indians and convince them that war is not necessary to enable them to obtain justice and that the United States have no desire to revenge the injuries they have received."

Pickering also expressed great delight that the Seneca had agreed to accept the "blessings of civilization." He made a long speech about this, to which the clear-eyed old Farmer's Brother made an eloquent reply. One of his jarring statements was that the western treaties were made with persons having no authority from their councils to sign away any Indian lands.

The old chief did not mention that the attack had been made in revenge for Indian attacks on the Ohio border, but Secretary Knox did. He replied, "All these wrongs have been done by both sides. Which side has done the most is hard to say without investigation. Let us begin anew!"

After the council had threshed out the problems that lay between the two parties, the Seneca agreed to visit the western tribes again and recommend peaceful settlements of differences. They also agreed to allow teachers to come among them and to permit the establishment of schools in several places. Red Jacket, once a principal opponent to such advances, now seemed to agree that schools might be a good thing, though later something happened to change his mind.

Everybody was happy at Philadelphia, even though two chiefs had died and had to be buried away from home. Grief was "wiped away"; the government passed a bill appropriating $1,500 annually for the purchase of a supply of clothing, animals, and farm implements for the Seneca. It was a generous amount then, and the Indians were happy with the outcome. They had been treated as equals and as members of an equally free state, so they thought. The American government had cause, also, to feel satisfaction. Here is how the feeling expressed itself: the Indians were to be given presents of new clothes!

Secretary Knox, accordingly, was instructed to give each chief a new military uniform, a cocked hat, and other military adornments. Red Jacket, among the rest, received his costume and a fine sword with gratitude. Then he laid the gifts aside.

"I am an advocate of peace," he said. "A military uniform and weapon do not become me. Not being a warrior, I would much prefer a plain suit."

"That is quite all right; we'll bring you one," said the quartermaster. In a short time the new suit was brought, tried on, and found to be a good fit.

"Hmm," remarked the quartermaster, "I'll take back the military uniform."

"Hmm," answered Red Jacket. "I am a man of peace, but I might find it necessary sometime to be a warrior. In that case I'll need a soldier's outfit."

"Hmm," said the quartermaster, turning on his heel.

"Hmm," said Red Jacket. "Somehow I have acquired two new suits."

He was learning rapidly, but there was still more in store for him. So well had he pointed out the reason for friction between the western Indians and the government and so eloquently had he spoken as the unchallenged leader of his delegation that George Washington had prepared another gift, one that could scarcely be forgotten.

The loyalty of Red Jacket to his promises of friendship with the United States was such that he never wore a George III medal; some Indians used the English medals as ornaments. To the orator the decoration was a symbol of allegiance, and he would have none rather than one that might be misleading. The appraising eyes of Secretary Knox had noted this, and with that observation came a suggestion. In due time the suggestion had become a fact.

"My brother," said George Washington as he faced Red Jacket, "I have here a token of my high regard for you and your people."

With this short statement the President unwrapped a large oval medal of silver. On one side was engraved the figure of the President extending his hand to a tall Indian smoking a peace pipe. In the distance was another Indian plowing with a yoke of oxen.

"Wear this, my brother," said the President, "and re-

member that my hand is ever extended to you in all efforts to bring the blessings of civilization and industry to
your people. Wear this because you are a friend of the
United States."

Such was the story that Red Jacket told when he returned home, quite overcome with the marked attention
paid him. His medal was worn always. When he died, it
passed to Jemmy Johnson, a Tonawanda chief sachem, and
from him to Donehogawa, who became the Grand Sachem
of the Six Nations. The original medal is now in the possession of the Buffalo Historical Society. There are other
medals of similar design, but Red Jacket's is the largest of
all. To him it was an enduring symbol of unswerving allegiance.

[9] *A TREATY*
TO END ALL TREATIES

FROM BEYOND THE Ohio to the land of the Seneca, runners
reported that Indian warriors were shouting, "We are free!
We are free! No white nation rules us." Red Jacket, hearing
this news, agreed that his people were under no other
nation's heel, and would make peace and seek friendship
where there was the best advantage. But, he warned the
Indian councils, American friendship, not British, offered
more security. The British were seeking Six Nations' support and wanted the Indians to do the fighting, he declared,

and when victory came, the British would claim the fruits. Washington, however, asked only for peace.

To such declarations Seneca war captains replied, "Yes, Washington promised us peace and friendship, but if his agents fail to keep their promises, we will take the guns the British offer us and fight the settlers who trespass."

The Seneca people agreed with the Miami, Ottawa, and Shawnee tribes that the Ohio River should be the final boundary line between the Americans on the east and the Indians on the west. This policy was strengthened when the confederated tribes living between the Ohio and Wabash rivers defeated two large bodies of American troops that had been sent to punish them. The American government was dismayed by this, and the Six Nations were disgusted. Couldn't Americans fight?

To make sure that there would be no other defeat, General Anthony Wayne took the field. He was grimly determined that, though the hostile Indians were aided by the British, American troops would outfight them and win.

The confederated Indians had another idea: if their chiefs Little Turtle and Blue Coat could muster enough warriors, General Wayne, "the Black Snake who never slept," might be caught off guard and overwhelmed. In this the support of a British garrison and equipment would count heavily for success. It was a case of Great Britain and the western Indians against a small army of resolute American backwoodsmen.

While General Wayne was watching his chance to attack the forces of Little Turtle, Colonel Pickering, knowing that the Six Nations at all cost must be given a satisfying agreement, invited them to hold a grand council with him. The place was to be Canandaigua, and the time September and October, 1794. To make sure that everyone should hear of the proposal, he sent messengers to all settlements of the Six Nations to invite chiefs, warriors, men, women, and children to attend the council.

"There will be presents for everybody," a messenger declared, "silver ornaments, dishes, beads by the yard, cloth, and needles."

"Yes," agreed another, "and there will be good times, music, parades, many feasts, dances, and games."

"Besides," the first messenger said, "the new town of the white men, Canandaigua, is like Philadelphia. It has new houses, some painted white, wide streets, stalls for horses, and stores where food and clothing may be bought. With Colonel Pickering to lead the council, you will be made secure at last, and we'll be friends forever."

Red Jacket always liked councils. They gave his fellow chiefs and himself a chance to air their grievances. If the council were held, lands lost through misunderstanding might be recovered. Then, without doubt, a new meekness would come over the American government—especially if Wayne were defeated—leaving Little Turtle to dictate the terms of peace. In any event, Red Jacket thought, a new treaty might settle boundary problems forever.

The chiefs were agreed that a good time for making a treaty was at hand. They wanted to be friendly with the Americans if possible, but they did hope to impress Pickering with their power to revenge American aggression. As the leaves were crisping on the trees in late September, fifteen hundred Seneca and Cayuga began to march toward the rising city of Canandaigua. They came from the territory that stretches between Kanadesaga and Sandusky and from the stream valleys of western New York. The departure of each group was timed to enable the several bands to reach the council grounds about the same time. The Indians, like children going to a fair, were in holiday mood, and even their leaders laid aside some of their sternness. It would be a gay time for autumn picnics, they thought; there would be new camps and large crowds. They were to see monster piles of new blankets, toys, bolts of cloth, scarves, kettles, knives, kegs of rum, and firkins of tobacco—all free!

Preparations had been made by each town of the Six Nations to dress for the occasion. Feathered bonnets, beaded dresses and leggings, and ornaments galore were dusted off and polished. Women had new baskets with brightly colored tops; craftsmen among the men had carved cups, ladles, bowls made from large burls or tree knots, and splint brooms made of white oak saplings. Well did they know that the curiosity-loving whites from the East liked such souvenirs.

Official runners shuttled back and forth to keep each town informed of what the other was doing so that, when the march was once under way, a grand appearance would be made. Thus, with new moccasins and clean shirts in their travel bags, blankets over their shoulders, and food in hampers, each group took up the journey to the "Chosen Town," as Canandaigua was called. The Seneca were coming from the West, and from the East the Oneida and the Onondaga. The Mohawk had not been invited because they no longer lived in New York. Brant, however, being an important influence, had an invitation from Pickering. He would be a watcher for the British, but the treaty commissioners felt that he could do little damage to American interests.

Advance parties of Indians had been sent to select camping sites and to erect cabins, tents, and bowers of branches and bark. Some camps were placed a mile or two from the village, some were on the shores of the lake, and others were near the top of the hill where the Canandaigua courthouse now stands. One was along Sucker Brook, where a clear stream of good water was an attraction.

Thus prepared, the groups took up their march, scuffling through the leaves and singing as the crisp autumn air raised their spirits. When they paused for rest during the day or overnight, camps were arranged in pine groves or under the wide-branched oaks that dotted the grasslands. Children frolicked; growing boys ran races, played lacrosse, shot their arrows, and chased rabbits. The journey was not a long one for any of the New York Indians, and it was a happy one. A trip of fifty to two hundred miles meant only pleasure.

Colonel Pickering knew that his invitation had been an agreeable one when in mid-October the friendly Oneida arrived and sang their songs of salutation in the council square. While they were yet making their presence known by ceremonial songs and dances, there came a faraway signal call. The cry sounded like that of a large army of warriors. Council scouts climbed trees to look westward and saw, instead of enemies, a long line of the Seneca led by a master of rites who carried a feathered spear. It was the first division of the tribe and was headed by Farmer's

Brother. Scouts, dressed in their finest costumes, walked before him, holding a wampum belt and a peace pipe and singing the ancient ambassadors' song. Even the Indians, accustomed to such ceremonial approaches, were impressed, and the whites who were fortunate enough to view the pageantry were greatly moved.

Farmer's Brother, tall and straight, was dressed as became a Seneca sachem. Every man in his party was robed in his finest blanket, his most colorful leggings, and his most decorative feathered cap. Many faces were painted with peace symbols, as in olden days, and all tomahawks were held in belts, not lifted as in war.

It was midafternoon before the pageantry of entrance had been completed and the company had been drawn up in a semicircle with the women and children behind. At the word *"oneh!"* there was utter silence, and at another signal a bevy of warriors stepped forward, lifted their muskets, aimed, and fired at the sky. This was repeated as a salute with three volleys. Then came the tribal cheer announcing safe arrival.

With ceremonies over, the principal chiefs shook hands with Colonel Pickering, General Chapin, and Thomas Morris. Pickering then welcomed the Seneca delegation in Indian style, and was addressed by Farmer's Brother who returned to him the wampum belt of invitation, a gesture that meant that the purposes of the conference would be met with frankness.

Quiet Quakers, seated or standing together at one side of the square, looked on with placid faces. They were eager to be helpful but refrained from making any move that would seem like intrusion. The Seneca had invited them and William Savery, their leader, as trusted friends. Red Jacket had heartily approved the invitation. He had wanted the Quakers to watch for any sharp practice that would defeat the best interests of the Indians.

Two days later Cornplanter, war chief of the Seneca, appeared with his escort from Allegany, and the ceremonial arrival and greetings were repeated. Then his company repaired to their camping spot, where each family sought to make itself comfortable.

On October 18 Red Jacket and his band of retainers arrived with their families. Though it appeared in ceremonial fashion, this band displayed less pomp than the others. After Red Jacket had greeted Colonel Pickering, he immediately inquired for William Savery and the Quakers. He wanted good advice before he made any statement.

After the arrival of Red Jacket's band, dinners were held for the chiefs, the Indians gave their dances and sang to amuse the crowd, and there was much visiting among the groups, all of which delayed the more serious work ahead.

One of the interruptions was a speech made by Jemimah Wilkinson, who had come to Canandaigua to call the Indians to repentance for their misdeeds. Her zealous plea soon became so overpowering that her sentences became a confused mixture of words that even the whites could not understand.

"Repent! Repent!" she cried.

The amazed Indian women looked on with wonder in their eyes. Here was a woman who wanted Indians to repent. They called Red Jacket aside and told him what they thought about her advice and what their answer would be.

"You, Red Jacket, answer for us," they requested. "It is not seemly for a woman to speak publicly."

The next day, fully primed, Red Jacket asked Colonel Pickering's permission to address the assembly. This being granted, the orator politely greeted the audience.

"On a previous day," he began, "we heard the thoughts of a lady of the palefaces. Now we ask that you hear the thoughts of our women. They instruct me to say that our sachems have spoken truly about how the white race has pressed and squeezed us together until we have a great pain in our hearts. We love our land, and we honestly think that those who have taken it away from us unjustly should return it very soon. One of your great women yesterday said that Indians should repent. In behalf of our women, we now call upon you of the white race to repent. You have as much need of repentance as we. Repent and wrong us no more!"

Red Jacket's message foreshadowed the concern that was felt by all. Once again, as before, Indians would be the victims of another agreement that would shrink the remaining acres of a people who once owned New York State from the Schoharie to Lake Chautauqua. To lose land and settlements meant that homes and gardens would have to go, and these had meant work. Little by little all incentive to improve any spot was being whittled down until the forlorn cry, "What's the use?" became general.

"Well, what did you think of the lady who called upon you to repent?" asked an interested inquirer.

Red Jacket is said to have repeated his usual answer to similar questions when there had been much talk.

He looked at his questioner, stroked his chin, wriggled his jaws violently, and then said in his halting English, "Too much, too much, too much cha, cha, cha, cha, cha!"

A day or so later, without announcement, a hitherto unknown delegate appeared. He was an alternate sent by Joseph Brant, who was unable to come. Brant could be endured, but not this stranger. Colonel Pickering was greatly displeased at the newcomer and believed him to be merely a spy sent by the Canadian British as a troublemaker. He denounced him and demanded his withdrawal.

"But I have come simply as a friendly representative of Captain Brant," the man said. "I am a Mohawk called William Johnson, Brant's alternate."

Cornplanter, astonished at Pickering's hostility, arose to defend his Mohawk friend, saying that no harm had been intended, since Johnson was a skilled interpreter.

"I seem to discover that, even after making a treaty of peace," said Cornplanter, "you Americans cannot bear to sit at the side of one with whom you have made the peace when treaty conferences with Indians are held. I know what is in our minds, for next spring we shall hold a grand council of tribes at Sandusky. Captain Brant has sent this representative to Canandaigua to say, 'You remember what we agreed upon last year and what boundary line we marked out. If this line is accepted, we will have peace. Before we go to Sandusky, we are invited to hold a preliminary council at Buffalo Creek.' This is what Captain Brant wishes to tell us here at Canandaigua."

The last thing that Colonel Pickering wanted to have brought up in any discussion with the Six Nations now was the question of the Ohio lands. He was furious, and if

Johnson were not a spy or agitator, at least he had come to introduce an unwelcome topic. Cornplanter had explained too much, thus tipping his hand.

"Johnson's intrusion is an impudent act," the colonel shouted, "and it gives fresh proof of British insolence!"

He continued his speech, shouting recriminations, and concluded by stating that his instructions from George Washington were to suffer no British agents to be present. Brant would have been considered merely a chief of the Mohawk nation.

Johnson was quite alarmed at the colonel's vehemence and withdrew quietly, whereupon Cornplanter spoke again.

"The council fire grows warm," he remarked. "The sparks fly about very thick. Let us have an intermission."

The tension soon eased, the colonel agreeing to furnish food for Johnson's return. That evening after the council had adjourned, Pickering invited the principal chiefs to have dinner with him, hoping to show that he was not hostile to them. Red Jacket, Cornplanter, Little Beard, Big Sky, and Fish Carrier were the honored guests.

Laying aside their hurt feelings and their reserve, these chiefs appeared at this dinner as most affable and even jolly. Red Jacket carried on a bantering conversation filled with good humor, and everyone laughed and sang together. It was a dinner, after all, not a council.

The next day, after the council had opened, a speaker for the Indians presented a letter of explanation addressed to Brant, expressing regret that Johnson had not been permitted to stay.

"We are determined to hold to the Ohio boundary

line," the letter said, concluding, "We find ourselves a poor and despised people, yet still independent, brought to suffering between two white nations striving which shall be the greater."

Pickering heard this letter with great indignation. He said so in a voice that did not conceal his anger, and the Indians were moved to equal anger that their right to send the letter had been questioned. The council was on the verge of dissolving, and words ran high.

At this juncture Red Jacket is said to have made his most brilliant speech. No accurate copy was made, but one author described the scene. "Rising gradually to his subject," the record states, "he delineated the primitive simplicity and happiness of his people, the wrongs they had sustained from the usurpation of the white man, with such a bold and beautiful pencil that every auditor was soon raised to vengeance, or melted to tears."

Upon hearing an interpretation of Red Jacket's remarks arguing against signing any treaty that ignored the demands of the Six Nations for the restoration of lands taken from them by sharp bargaining, many of the white people became alarmed, fearing a hostile outbreak. The Indians intended no such measure.

Red Jacket knew that the Indians were saddened by the expulsion of Brant's spokesman and by the angry rejection of proposals that lands be returned to the Six Nations. He endeavored to spur his people to a greater courage, more self-respect, and caution. He was trying to raise their patriotism, and he did. After his speech, which Pickering had deplored, the Indians whispered among themselves that maybe, after all, the defeat of General

Wayne would alter the views of Pickering and make him less severe. If Little Turtle could win, the position of the Six Nations and the Americans would be reversed.

Then came one of those unexpected climaxes that bring both good fortune and tragedy.

A runner appeared in the distance, shouting a cry of distress. "News, news, unhappy news," he signaled.

Everyone was startled by this interruption, and then with mixed feelings they saw him dash into a group of chiefs.

"News from the West," he cried. "Wayne, 'the Black Snake,' has whipped Little Turtle and all his allies. All have scattered in defeat; the power of the western confederates has been broken!"

The effect of this news was immediate and brought dismay. The hitherto arrogant Seneca and their brethren were suddenly deflated. It is possible that some even felt a growing fear that now the government of the United States might impose far harsher conditions upon the Indians. Now there was no military threat to ensure the white man's respect. Wayne's victory at this critical moment had tipped the scales for Pickering.

The American commissioners were now able to present in concise terms just what they wanted. Their general declaration was that "peace and friendship" were the desired aims. After that the United States wanted each nation of the six to recognize and accept definite boundaries and to understand to whom, and to whom only, they might sell their land when they wished to sell. To outlaw private feuds between Indians and whites, the commissioners said that hereafter punishment should be ad-

ministered by American law. Better still, the lands
described as belonging to the Six Nations were to be
theirs "for their free use and enjoyment thereof, but it shall
remain theirs until they choose to sell to the people of the
United States, who have the right to purchase." Even better was the statement, "The United States will never
claim the same, nor disturb the Seneca nor any of the Six
Nations." Not so good was the proposal that the Six Nations would never claim any other lands. Other things
were stipulated, such as permission for the people of the
United States to pass freely through Indian lands.

All these proposals were introduced by a sentence that
gave the Six Nations great heart, notwithstanding, for it
appealed to their pride as a presumably independent nation. It said, "Peace and friendship are hereby firmly established and shall be perpetual between the United
States and the Six Nations."

To the Indians it meant but one thing, that the United
States considered the Six Nations an organized government on a par with itself and that the two nations, being
on equal terms, could make a treaty defining for the first
time in the history of the Six Nations their rights and land
boundaries.

As an inducement for the Indians to accept American
proposals, Colonel Pickering opened the treasure house of
gifts. Here was a quantity of goods valued at $10,000, all
to be given freely to the red men. In addition to all former
amounts agreed to be given, the American agents promised
that $4,500 would be expended by the government each
year forever for the benefit of the Six Nations and their
descendants. (Today these Indians number about six

thousand, and the annual amount given each, therefore, is about seventy-five cents.)

The season was growing late and the winds of early winter were beginning to blow, making life in the temporary camps disagreeable. The Indians wanted to go home, and the women complained about the delay in reaching an agreement. Pickering, himself, was anxious to complete the work of the council and return to Philadelphia with a signed treaty.

"Let us cheerfully agree," he urged the Indians. "Join me in digging a deep pit in which to bury all former differences and take hold of the chain of friendship so tightly that nothing will force it from our hands."

Red Jacket had been appointed to make a reply, and he did so in a long, serious speech. "We, too, are a soft-hearted people," he said, "and we desire peace with you. We unite with you in holding a chain of friendship that shall link us together, and may that chain remain forever bright."

Encouraged by Red Jacket's response, Colonel Pickering explained in a friendly manner that the United States wanted roadways through Indian lands, and for this privilege would grant the Indians all the lands upon which their villages stood. This was a concession he had determined earlier not to make because of former Indian raids.

There was more argument, more effort by the Indians to hold on to rights they valued, but it was of no avail. The treaty was flashed before them, a finished product. This document was not of their making nor drafted by their own agents, but it was the treaty demanded.

It was signed, and among its signatures appear the names of fifty-nine authorized chiefs, the second one being Handsome Lake. These men were presumably authorized to sign a treaty. Toward the end, with Farmer's Brother, Big Kettle, and Cornplanter, appears the Indian name of Red Jacket; it was badly misspelled.

The United States at last had settled its long misunderstandings with the Six Nations, and now these Indians had something that should be their own forever until they should "choose to sell." The method by which they could be made to choose to sell was a matter not mentioned.

Let us now look at the more human side of the position of the Indians while at Canandaigua. We have mentioned their camp sites but have said nothing about how the people lived. We should know that each camp at once had organized its hunting parties, its fishermen, and its cooks. Hunters scoured the adjacent hills for deer, frequently bringing in a hundred or more every day. Fish and small game furnished the variety that was needed.

The autumn air was crisp, and at all times the pleasant smoke of numerous fires could be seen and smelled. At night a myriad of lights dotted the forest, and some on elevations could be seen for quite a distance. In every cluster of huts there were group singing, drumming, the sound of rattles, and sometimes the mournful notes of the cedar flute. Folk songs and legends were told about the fires, and there were numerous shouts of sheer joy mingled with the laughter of children.

William Savery in his journal gives us a picture of the scene as it appeared to him. An extract from his diary will be sufficient:

Fifth Day, Oct. 30. After dinner John Parrish and myself
rode to the Farmer's Brother's encampment, which contained
about five hundred Indians. They are located by the side of a
brook in the woods; having built about seventy or eighty huts,
by far the most commodious and ingeniously made I have seen.

The principal materials [for the houses] are bark and boughs
of trees, so nicely put together as to keep the family dry and
warm. The women as well as the men appear mostly employed.
In this camp there are a large number of pretty children, who
in all activity and buoyancy of health, were diverting themselves according to their fancy. The vast number of deer they
have killed since coming here, which they cut up, and hang
round their huts inside and out to dry, together with the ra-
tions of beef which they draw daily, gives the appearance of
plenty to supply the few wants to which they are subjected.

Savery mentions no evidence that the Indians were
dejected or fearful, howsoever their politicians might
wrangle with the commissioners and recite their woes.
Among themselves at home they seemed to be a happy,
contented, and even jocular people. Savery mentions this
as he continues:

The ease and cheerfulness on every countenance and the
delightfulness of the afternoon, which these inhabitants of the
woods seem to enjoy with a relish far superior to those who are
pent up in crowded and populous cities, all combined to make
this the most pleasant visit I have made to Indians; and induced
me to believe that before they became acquainted with white
people and were infected with their vices, they must have been
as happy as any people in the world.

Savery and Parrish had seen enough for a time and
turned their horses about to return. Savery says of this,
"In returning to our quarters we passed by the Indian
council, where Red Jacket was displaying his oratory to

his brother chiefs on the subject of Colonel Pickering's proposals."

Soon after this visit to the Indian camp, Red Jacket called on Savery, perhaps to thank him for help and advice. "Red Jacket," wrote Savery, "visited us with his wife and five children, whom he had brought to see us. They were exceedingly well clad, in their manner, and the best behaved and prettiest children I have ever met with."

Such is a fleeting picture not often presented. These people, fifteen hundred of them, must now return to their homes. The treaty had been signed, and they were laden with gifts. Outwardly everything was the same as before except that now each knew just what he could expect to call his own. They were happy in the thought that now there would be no disturbance. They were at peace, believing that they could hold their lands until they chose to sell, and that meant they would never so choose.

They took their departure, singing in ceremonial fashion as they left the vale of the lake to follow the western slopes of the hills down to the Genesee and then onward to the lands of their nation—Tonawanda, Cattaraugus, and Allegany. All was theirs now, forever—maybe!

[10] *NEVER SHALL YOU*
KNOW WANT AGAIN

THOUGH RED JACKET had signed the Canandaigua treaty, he was not happy. He had signed it only because a majority of the chiefs had agreed to it and thereby made unanimous approval a required act. He had voiced his disapproval, and if disturbances followed, no one could blame him for not having warned his people. The treaty stated that the Indians should not be "disturbed," but Red Jacket knew that, as long as land was wanted, intrusion and offers to buy would follow.

With his wife and little children, he now tramped the muddy autumn trails back to the valley of the Genesee, crossing at Canawaugus (opposite the present Avon), wending the rougher trail to Big Spring (Caledonia), walking the Big Bend of the Tonawanda, and thence to Tonawanda Indian village, where he had relatives. It was a journey of about seventy-five miles, and with the children it took three days. Such walks were not unusual, and in the brisk November air, with the forests and grasslands yielding the aroma of Indian summer, the beauties of the woodland and stream did not go unnoticed. Red Jacket was ever a lover of nature, and he often stopped to view some detail that caught his attention. Arriving at the village of Tonawanda, he paused with his family to view the falls and try his skill at bass fishing. He laughed when he found one of his old poles hidden in a tree. Tonawanda Falls was an ancient camping site once occupied by a mysterious tribe that made arrowheads. Red Jacket knew where the flint might be found and visited the cliffs from which it had been dug. He told his children how the water sprites had made holes in the bed of the creek above the falls so that they could pound seeds into meal. These holes were about the size of an apple and quite round. He lit his pipe and blew smoke at them for luck.

When the Seneca were back in their villages, they began to discuss with great seriousness what had happened to them.

"Notice this," observed Red Jacket. "Our lines have shrunk. Once our boundary ran from Oneida Lake down the Unadilla. Now it is on the Genesee River. What will happen next?"

"I will object with all my force," answered Young King (a nephew of Old King), "if anyone wants our land between the Genesee River and Chautauqua. We must hold it."

"I think we are not wary enough," put in Little Billy. "The white man can say things that we do not understand; we ought to understand more, just as George Washington said."

"Henry O'Bail, he says things," said Young King, speaking of Cornplanter's son. "He says that in Philadelphia the white people believe that, if we do not use the land, we should not hang on to it and that, if we do try to keep it without using it, smart men will come along and take it away."

"We have no lands to sell anybody!" stormed Red Jacket. "We love our land; it is our hunting ground. How shall we have meat without it?"

"Henry O'Bail says we should raise more corn, raise cows, have pigs," said Young King. "I think it would be good for us."

"You will soon be thinking that preachers will be good for us," said Red Jacket.

"I never noticed that they harmed us any," replied Young King.

Conversations like this were long reported by the missionaries who came among the friendly Seneca. They later made numerous converts, although Red Jacket could not understand why.

"We have our own way, given to us by the Great Spirit," he would say. "Missionaries come, and after them the gamblers [land buyers], and with them all is lost."

"Cornplanter doesn't believe missionaries mean our destruction," said Young King. "Even he learns from the

Quakers and is friendly with preachers. Black Coats are very kind," observed Young King.

"You'll become a Christian yet!" exclaimed Red Jacket, scorning any good word about the Black Coats.

"I might," answered Young King, and many years later he did.

During the closing months of 1794, the Seneca gave more thought to their own customs than they had for some years. The masters of religious rites were more active than ever, seeking to awaken the drooping spirits of the younger people, who were becoming disobedient and heedless of the old ceremonies.

To the older people and many of the joy-loving youths, the rhythm of the ceremonies of the long houses was a soul-warming experience. It was a pleasure to worship and to join in the thanksgiving rituals. Only a few sneering warriors scoffed at their elders and called them "pagans." That was a word heard in the taverns, and it was uttered in ridicule.

During midwinter, 1795, the new year ceremony was held at all the long houses throughout the land of the Six Nations. At Buffalo Creek the council lodge was crowded to the doors, and for nine days and nights there were songs, dances, marches, and sermons filled with advice by the Keepers of the Faith. Masked members of the Order of the False Faces came into the building and performed their rites. They were willing to heal certain ailments and blew ashes through the hair of their patients to scare away disease. In secret places back among the trees, the Company of the Little Water held its ceremonies. The members sat around their long house, chanting their rites all night, shaking gourd rattles, and listening for sounds of the animals of the unseen world who were believed to guard them from harm. The Little Water group was sometimes called "They who guard us." Most of the forest birds and animals used for food were honored by dances because the Seneca believed that all living things had souls. "Didn't the same Creator make them? Are they not our lesser brothers? Their spirits must be made to know that the human race is very grateful and will not kill them wantonly." Thus did the Keepers of the Faith instruct their children.

There was a society for most of these helpful creatures. There was the Company of the Pigeons, the Company of the Eagles, the Society of the Mystic Animals, the Bear Society, the Buffalo Society, and many others. Even the young people could become members if they could qualify. Girls and women could join a society which was organized to express thanks for corn and bread. They had a cheerful dance and used box tortoise shells for their rattles.

Possibly one of the most dramatic of ceremonies at Buffalo Creek and along the Genesee was the sacrifice of the white dogs. White dogs without blemish were considered fit friends of man to go to the spirit world to report to the Creator what men had done and how mankind had shown gratitude for the blessings of the universe. Strangled, covered with ornaments and wampum, these sacrificial dogs were hung upon poles for several days. At an appointed time they were placed on a low altar and burned. As the smoke ascended, a master of rites would chant a long thanksgiving, expressing the gratitude of the people. When this ceremony had been performed, the faithful took strings of white wampum in their hands and resolved to make their lives better. One by one each repentant person would walk a straight path that had been drawn far out in the snow and confess his sins to the unseen powers of the universe. The Seneca did not believe that these powers could be sinned against, for they were too great to be injured by man. They thought that men sinned against other men and that, to overcome the wrongs done, they must confess in sorrow, repent, and make restitution for all damages done to others. If one stole, he must return more than he took. If he lied, he must tell the truth publicly.

As Red Jacket joined in the rites of his faith, he found the inspiration to continue his efforts to protect his people. His religion was to him a precious inheritance.

"We also have a religion," he told a missionary who was inviting his people to change their beliefs. "It teaches us to be kind."

He might have added that, though Christians regarded Indians as pagans, no Indian ever swore. The invention of profane language was beyond their pagan minds.

When the season of the new year (the first moon after mid-January) passed, discussion by the chiefs about the future of their race was renewed. What was its future? What more would the whites demand?

For two years this question was raised in councils, and its only possible answer was, "More!" Influential white citizens who came as visiting advisers reminded the chiefs and sachems that all had not been settled. There was still another emergency to face, that of the rights of Robert Morris. This great Philadelphia merchant and patriot had bought the surrendered Phelps-Gorham rights to land lying west of the Genesee. It was some time before the full meaning of this claim was realized by the Seneca people and their leaders.

Morris, needing funds, had sold his right to the lands to the Holland Land Company. He received an advance payment, but the full amount would not be forthcoming until he had paid the Indians for any rights they might have. Time had gone on with Morris putting off any attempt to deal with the Indians until the way had been paved for a settlement without inciting them to war. Now he could no longer delay, for the Holland company was pressing him for completed delivery of title to the land. To do this, he must persuade the Seneca owners to release to him all their claims to the land. Under the law it was Massachusetts land, but the Indians still lived upon it.

The Seneca scarcely realized the character of this strangle hold but felt that it might have been a natural part of their own dangerous position as onetime allies of the British. Yet they loved what they had, and not one ever thought of selling an acre.

Then came a shock. Agents of Robert Morris began to "disturb" them again. These men visited the chiefs in a friendly way and finally announced that a grand council would be held at Big Tree on the Genesee. Presents were lavish and rum flowed. The agents were good fellows who talked of "the best interests of the people," how unfortunate it was to have bad white people all around them, and how much better the Seneca would be if they had plenty of money to buy the "blessings of civilization." If now the Seneca would come to Big Tree, they would see presents piled higher than ever before. There would be a happy time, and everybody would profit.

The time set for the gathering was August 25, 1797. But Indians began to come more than a week in advance of the formal opening, for food in abundance had been promised.

When the Seneca had finally gathered on the grassy plain east of the Genesee, Thomas Morris, son of Robert, began to present his arguments. Yes, frankly, his father did want the land and would pay a great price for it—a very great price.

"An annual income from the sale of the portions of your territory that you are not actually living on," he said, "will be better for you than retaining a large tract of country from which you can derive no benefit, save for use as hunting grounds; but you may still hunt on these grounds even if you do sell them."

At this carefully worded offer, the Seneca looked at each other in amazement. They had never suggested selling the land. Was it for their benefit that this land was to be sold, or for the benefit of the buyer? Indeed they were deeply disturbed by the proposal.

The agitation of each group in the tribe was noticeable. The warriors, women, chiefs, and sachems were in an uproar. It required all the diplomacy of young Morris to keep matters running smoothly. After a temporary halt the council was reopened for more discussion.

As the proposal stood, it was entirely legal. In accord with previous agreement a delegate from Massachusetts was present, and Jeremiah Wadsworth represented the government. These commissioners had attended in order to see that the Indians were not cheated.

Red Jacket was outwardly calm for a while, and then he spoke. He said that his people were not convinced that it was their duty to sell their rights at any price. The consciousness of owning these beautiful stretches of level land with their forests and their streams was a matter of importance to the Seneca nation, he said. "Mr. Morris thinks otherwise, but we owe it to our self-respect to have a territory we can call our own."

"To own such a territory means everything to us," he shouted, his voice ringing far over the council grounds. "It raises us in our own estimation, it creates in our bosoms a proud feeling that elevates a nation. Observe the difference between the estimation in which a Seneca and an Oneida are held. We are courted, while the Oneida are considered a degraded people fit only to make brooms and baskets. Why this difference? It is because the Seneca are known as proprietors of a broad domain, while the Oneida are cooped up in a narrow space."

Mr. Morris in replying told the Indians that the Seneca were not as important as they thought. If so, the western Indians would have paid more attention to their advice when they counseled Little Turtle and his Miami warriors to seek peace rather than war.

"It is quite true," answered Red Jacket, "that our reception was cold. That happened because we were in the bad company of white commissioners whom the western Indians would not trust. The commissioners did not help the cause of the United States."

When some of the Indians pressed Morris for the price he was willing to give, he weighed the objections of the Seneca against the topmost amount his father could afford to pay. Finally he answered that he would give $100,000 for the 4 million acres plus the presents he had brought.

"Let us sell you one township for a dollar an acre," replied a sachem. "You can easily sell the land for five dollars an acre and make a profit of four dollars. That's our proposal."

"Impossible!" exclaimed Morris, flying into a rage.

William Bayard of the Holland company here took Morris aside and advised him to frighten the Indians by telling them that, if this was the best that could be done, there was little use in continuing the discussion. Morris received this suggestion with doubts, but, to satisfy the Holland buyer, he repeated Bayard's words to the Seneca.

Red Jacket now sprang to his feet, his face wreathed in smiles. "Brother," he exclaimed, "you have arrived at the point I wished to bring you. You told us in your first address that, in the event of our not agreeing to sell our land, we should part friends." He paused and looked at Morris. Then, dramatically extending his hand, he said, "Here then is my hand. I now cover the council fire."

Morris and the Holland representative were completely taken aback. They began to fear bodily harm, for Morris had fallen directly into Red Jacket's trap.

The Indians roared their approval, shouting with delight and whooping as if a victory had been won. Many sang, and an impromptu war dance was started, the drums sounding ominously.

It took some time and a vast amount of bribery to bring about a reopening of the council. Confidential agents circulated among the Indians, slyly whispering promises of great personal wealth, presents, free rum, and a jolly good time if the Seneca would listen again and agree.

Robert Morris had foreseen that objections might stall the agreement and in a letter, now on file among the Morris papers, told his son Thomas that, if need be, annuities could be promised the chiefs and sachems who would agree to the sale. The amounts were to be from a hundred to a thousand dollars a year, according to the importance of the chief or sachem.

Thus, when the treaty agents privately told the war chiefs that the deal would be forced through no matter what happened, that the government had a way of getting what it wanted, and that, if they would not agree, they would lose good life incomes already set aside for them, the fickle chiefs yielded to the reopening of the council.

When the meeting was called again, the sachems who had opposed any thought of selling land felt a sting of defeat. The sachems, the civil leaders, did not "choose to sell" to anyone. But at this point the work of the white agents revealed itself. The women of the Seneca suddenly declared a revolt against the authority of the sachems and placed the war chiefs in supreme authority.

"It is we, the women, who own the land," they affirmed. "Our warriors defend it. No longer will we listen to the advice of old men who only sit and smoke their pipes. Our warriors shall make the decision!"

The sachems and some of the more able war chiefs, scarcely believing their ears, were astonished by this revolt of the women, but sachems owed their offices to the women, who could depose them for any cause. What had brought about this violent change of front?

It was the solemn promise of Thomas Morris to the women that, if they agreed to the sale, they never should know want again.

Morris was now able to face the Indian council and say to them, "Never again will so large an amount as $100,000 be offered you for this land by anyone."

There were more than 4 million acres, which covered the richest area of the state. Cities now stand upon this land, and it is obvious that scores of later buyers would have outbid such a price. Yet Morris assured his hearers that no one who would offer so much would ever be found. Under the Canandaigua treaty the Seneca had the right to "choose to sell." It seemed to many of them that the time to make such a choice had come.

The warriors looked at each other and wondered what would happen if they, like the sachems, stood against this deal. The President of the United States was for it; the title was not theirs—only the right of occupancy. If the whites wanted the land, no promise would stop them. An army like that which whipped Little Turtle might come. The loss was inevitable. Against this were annuities for life; annuities meant ease and no more worries. The war chiefs wavered.

"One hundred thousand dollars!" said Morris. "This money can ensure that not only you but your children and your children's children will derive from it a lasting benefit. It can be placed in the Bank of the United States, from whence a sufficient income can annually be drawn by the President, your father, to make you and your posterity happy forever. Then the wants of your old and poor can be supplied, and in times of scarcity the women and children of your nation can be fed. You will no longer experience the miseries resulting from nakedness and want."

This alluring promise is found in the records of the Morris transaction, probably written by Thomas himself. It was his argument. The bid was such a strong one that it could scarcely be topped. Freedom from want at such a small price was a goal which few people of the world had ever attained. The money would be placed in the Bank of the United States and would "grow," and there would be prosperity forever.

Then the warriors and hunters were attracted by the promise (with no strings attached to it then) that the hunting rights would be unimpaired. They thought this over, "wealth forever, no more poverty, hunting rights forever." What more could any people want? It was true security!

In passing, it is sad but important to observe that no such promises were included in the written text of the Big Tree treaty. To the Indians, words given by voice were as sacred as those written down, and they totally forgot that this might not be the white man's way of looking at the subject later on.

With the still-objecting sachems, stubborn but overruled, the women now would prevail. At once Morris called a special council of the women. Perhaps, he said, the women had been kept in ignorance of what he had promised and the liberality of his offer, which, Morris repeated, was particularly made to relieve the distress of the women and the children. Since the women had had no part in the ill treatment he had received, he would give them the presents he had brought. Thomas Morris's own record states that he "begged them [the women] to contrast their present situation with the one they would be placed in if furnished with money enough to provide the comforts of life." He ended his plea by presenting them with strings of wampum to remind them, "whenever thereafter they experienced the hardships of poverty, to show the strings to their sachems and tell them with that belt they had been offered wealth" which had been rejected. Morris added in his record of the event, "This had an excellent effect on the women [who] at once declared themselves for selling, and the business began to wear a better aspect."

To understand the history of these people after the Treaty of Big Tree, it is important to realize that there were three Indian councils of equal power. The women had the greatest power, since they could set aside the decisions of the sachems, or civil chiefs. Next came the sachems' council, long respected and generally regarded as the most important council of the men. Its members came into office by the nomination of the women, and the title of sachem was hereditary. Then there was a council of the war chiefs, the military men. In war and in village leadership, these war chiefs were independent of the sachems. Their council could even declare war without the authority of their government.

Thus, when an emergency of divided opinion arose and the problem of selling the land for permanent security and freedom from want forever became the issue, the women of the Seneca nation revolted, disclaimed the authority of their sachems, and then and there constituted the council of war chiefs the governing body.

Morris had been skilled in the art of dividing and winning. He had lived with the Indians and knew their customs. He knew also that, when goods or wealth had been set aside for Indians, they would believe it to be rightly theirs and claim it. It was, therefore, easy to offer bribes to the weaker chiefs and then to demand that they agree to sell their land. The land buyer, following the trend of the times and the belief that the Indians were doomed anyway, merely used the resources at his disposal to gain his ends. He took from ignorance and weakness what he could get for a pittance.

When it became known throughout the camps at Big Tree what the Seneca women had done, Red Jacket was found unconscious beneath a tree, where he remained in a stupor for some time. However, when he recovered and learned that the majority of chiefs had opposed the sachems and had agreed to sign, he dutifully made the treaty unanimous by placing his own name on the document. The old custom was that, if most agreed, all should agree. He also asked for his pound of flesh in the form of an annuity for life. He was awarded $300 a year.

In this manner a territory of many square miles, stretching from the Genesee River to the western boundary of the state, was acquired for the price of two and one-half cents an acre. Only a few small areas along the Genesee were retained by the Seneca. Larger areas along the Allegheny River, Tonawanda Creek, and Cattaraugus Creek, with a square mile at an oil spring, were made "reservations" where the Seneca might continue to live under their own laws and regulations. To this day they hold their larger tracts and refuse to be tempted again. They discovered that "security forever" meant only a yearly income of a little over two dollars. For this they had bartered a paradise.

Once back upon their remaining lands, the Indians again recounted what had happened to them. At Buffalo Creek the chiefs met for a discussion, as usual talking it over after a treaty had been made irrevocable.

"I was against it from the start," declared Young King, who now had succeeded his uncle Old King and had become a leading chief at Buffalo.

"I, too, was against this sale," mournfully added Farmer's Brother, "but the women—look what they did!"

At this Red Jacket sprang to his feet and called for attention. "*Dasahtondah!*" he exclaimed, meaning "Do thou listen." He stood fiery-eyed, facing his fellow chiefs. "What has been promised by the trickery of words," he exclaimed, "cannot be fulfilled. Do you believe we shall have all that was promised by the agents? We shall never get it. Our kettles will be worn out, our cloth will be rags, the women's cows will have turned skinny and have died, and our jewelry will have turned green before many days. When the last slab of bacon is gone, we shall have found out that we have eaten up our land. But we may hunt as before, you say? That, too, is a promise that will not be honored, for the settlers will have hewn down the forests and frightened away all game."

His words were true.

[11] *A PROPHET APPEARS*

FOR MORE THAN a decade before the Big Tree treaty, settlers had been coming into the fertile region east of the
Genesee. By 1789 small hamlets and clusters of farms were
being established in old Indian clearings or in spots where
trade and milling seemed to promise rewards.

By the time of the Pickering treaty (1794), Canandaigua, Bath, Geneva, Poultneyville, Lyons, and Williamsburg were becoming thriving centers in the wilderness.
Williamsburg, however, petered out soon after 1805. The
town of Geneseo was its successful rival.

Farther west at the mouth of Buffalo Creek, New Amsterdam, as Buffalo was first named, was becoming a lake port and a gathering place for adventurers. For a long time, however, its future depended on the good will of the Seneca.

In the lands which Phelps and Gorham had purchased, real-estate offices were opened, roads were built over the narrow Indian trails, and traffic began to move east and west over mud sloughs that passed for highways. The Indians had sullenly given up their claims to this country east of the Genesee, but as if they had sent a ghostly punishment for their losses, a terrifying enemy threatened the fortunes of the new land. The people fell sick with a malady called "Genesee fever," burning and shaking by turns until they wasted away to mere shadows. It was believed to be caused by something bad in the air, something called "miasma." The disease was thus sometimes known as malaria, which means "bad air."

One of Red Jacket's favorite tall stories was about a traveler who, while passing along the Genesee road, heard a voice calling from a barn. The traveler could see nothing but a shadow but, upon going closer, thought he saw the outlines of a man.

"Hello," he cried, "is anybody there?"

"Yep, I'm here, but maybe ye can't see me because I've had the shakes so long and can't get rid of them."

"Bless my soul," said the traveler. "Here's a drink o' medicine; take it and I'll watch it run down ye."

"Thankee," said the shadow, taking a swallow.

"Blimy," said the traveler afterward, "if the shadder didn't walk away."

Tales like this were frequently swapped by the Indians

and whites, but even the heavy toll of malaria did not seem to stop the flow of settlers. Many of them were veterans of Sullivan's campaign who had seen the land and had found it far better than any they had seen before.

The sprawling towns that had sprung up had many things the Indians wanted. There were food and drink, especially strong drink, for which they had acquired a taste. Taverns lured them, and many red men became drunkards, diseased, shiftless, and dirty. Their old spirit was broken, and what they saw of white civilization gave them little encouragement. In their weakened state they became easy prey of gamblers and speculators in furs and often were badly abused. They had dropped low in the scale of self-respect.

Conscientious white people tried to help. The Quakers were especially kind, taking a number of Indian boys and girls to Philadelphia where they might live in good homes and attend schools. One of the boys was Henry O'Bail, the son of Cornplanter and nephew of Handsome Lake. He learned to read the Bible and became a student of its teachings, but he did not follow them, though he liked to argue about them.

Springtime had come to the Allegany country where Cornplanter lived. It was 1799, two years after Big Tree, and many of the Allegany Seneca were beginning to come out of the woodlands where they had been cutting trees and peeling bark. Logs were dragged to the swollen river and tied into rafts, which the Indians guided toward Pittsburgh. It was a rough voyage, and most of these tough and tousled red men drank heavily as they bucked the wind and river. Some were drowned. Others who had returned celebrated with sprees, yelling so loudly and brandishing tomahawks so violently that the people of the village of Burnt Houses became frightened and fled into the woods for protection.

In a small shack near Burnt Houses lay a babbling invalid, delirious and wasted to a mere skeleton. He was a pitiful victim of malaria and its so-called "cure," rum. In his fevered ravings he began to express his repentance for his sins.

"Great Spirit, give me strength to walk again, if this is Your will," he prayed, doing this as he had been told that white people did.

In a quavering voice and in almost inaudible syllables, he sang some of the sacred songs of his religion, the songs of the spirits, the harvest song, the song of gratitude for the corn. When he stopped for breath, he murmured, "Evil has befallen all of us because of the strong drink; it has laid me low."

That night he slept fitfully, and his needs were supplied by his faithful daughter. Through the night she heard him murmuring as if talking to unseen beings, but before morning he was quiet.

Next day his dimming eyes looked out at the late May sunshine, and he breathed a sigh of gratitude. "The Creator made this sunshine," he said, and then he shut his eyes again.

Soon afterward, while both his daughter and her husband were sitting on the doorstep, they heard him speak as if conversing with someone.

"*Nyuh,*" he replied to some inaudible voice, "I'll do it!"

Then they heard him rise from his bed and shuffle toward the door. Quickly the daughter sprang up, but only to see her father totter. She caught his withered form just as he crumpled to the floor. With her husband's help the limp figure was carried back to his rude bed.

The bereft daughter stood upon the doorstep and gave the wail that told of the death of a relative. Neighbors heard the cry and passed the news along.

"Speed your way," said the grieving Yewenot to her husband Hatgwiyot. "Find Cornplanter and Awl Breaker and tell them that Handsome Lake is dead."

In response Awl Breaker, a chief of distinction, came to the lodge of mourning, but Cornplanter, the half brother of Handsome Lake, continued his hoeing until the field was finished.

The house soon filled with sympathizing neighbors, and even the drunken raftsmen sobered up to keep the peace while death lay within a mourner's lodge. After all, Handsome Lake was a sachem; he had been an able adviser.

Awl Breaker, as he looked at the silent form, began to wonder about the strange look on Handsome Lake's face. He seemed to be watching something, perhaps even speaking in his sleeping mind. Awl Breaker bent over the stiffened body and placed his hand over the heart.

"Hold back your wails," he said. "Our sachem is not dead and may rise again. Let us watch and be patient."

Running his hand over the body, Awl Breaker felt the shrunken flesh respond, though few would believe him. How could a skeleton like that be alive? Near relatives continued to mourn, thinking revival impossible.

About noon the watchful Awl Breaker saw the lips of

the "dead man" move as if talking. Warm blood was puls-
ing now in his chest and could be felt at his back. Awl
Breaker spoke to the silent figure, asking, "My uncle, have
you recovered?"

To the astonishment of everyone the shrouded figure
answered, "I believe that I have recovered."

Though manifestly weak, he spoke with seeming assurance, exclaiming, "Never before have I seen such won-
drous visions!"

The erstwhile mourners pressed against the walls of the
shack and listened. Not another voice interfered.

"First I thought I heard someone speaking," said Handsome Lake. "I thought it was only my sickness, and when
asked if I would come to the door, I replied, 'Nyuh!' Yet the
voices seemed very real, and I arose to go to the door.
There before me were three men, with a fourth indis-
tinctly behind. These men were in fine, clean raiment, and
their faces were painted red, as if it had been done the day
before. Never before have I seen such commanding men.
In their hands they held bows, carried like canes, and they
bore sprigs of huckleberry bushes with berries of all
colors."

His eyes were open now, and Handsome Lake turned his
head to look at the crowd with eyes that were very bright.
He paused and then resumed his account.

"The four beings told me," he testified, "that they had
been sent to me by He Who made us. Then they told me to
take the berries and eat them as medicine for my restoration."

He proceeded to tell what medicine people he would
consult and how one draft of their brew would cause new

strength to come to him. The story, as preserved by the Seneca, tells how he took the medicine, how he gained his strength, and how he soon was able to call a council, at which he told of his marvelous visions, all witnessed in the few hours of his unconsciousness.

In a newly vibrant voice, Handsome Lake told of his call to the service of his people and how he had been instructed to give them word of the better way of life.

"I shall receive other instructions," he asserted, "and through the words of the four messengers my people shall know the will of our Creator."

It was not long after that, that Handsome Lake, now appearing in the guise of a prophet, proclaimed that the Creator had revealed to him the four great offenses that lay at the base of all Indian misery. However, there were also other forms of misconduct which should be avoided. The great offenses were strong drink, witchcraft, gambling, and secret poisoning, but reluctance to have children, unfaithfulness to one's mate, fiddle dancing, and card playing were also evil.

In his messages to the now aroused people, he analyzed the peculiar sins of Indians, and with these sins denounced, he called upon everyone immediately to forswear them. He even gave the formulas by which to seek forgiveness. Of all sins, drunkenness was the worst, but such things as trying to live exactly like white people in a spirit of pride were also denounced. A well-chosen code of morals was delivered as the pattern that all must now follow. It had been revealed that there was a new heaven and a new way to reach it, and if any faltered or failed, there was a new place of punishment where sinners would be punished forever according to their misdeeds. Only virtue, kindness to one's neighbor, faithfulness to the Creator combined with utter gratitude, and devotion to approved ceremonies would find favor with the Great Spirit.

With his role as a prophet came that of a teacher. He envisioned things that were to come, and he foresaw conditions that were not dreamed about. The loss of Buffalo Creek reservation was predicted. "Truly, this reservation will fall to the white man," he said. "The four messengers have revealed it."

Then he reported a vision about which many have smiled and which brought scorn from many Indians. It was a thing that couldn't happen. Handsome Lake said that, pointing to the sky, the four messengers had commanded him, "Watch! Look upon the eastern heavens and observe! What do you see there?"

"I replied that I saw two immense spheres, like colored liquid, and it seemed as if they were suspended only for an instant and were about to fall. One was red and one was yellow."

" 'Truly you have spoken,' answered the four messengers. 'If one should fall, there would be great calamity throughout the earth. Many people would leave the earth should one fall, but we the four messengers are doing our utmost to prevent such a calamity!' "

Apparently the balls did not fall, but calamity would come, nevertheless, in the white man's year of 2010, for the messengers said that mankind would then perish from the earth.

The Prophet declared that many other revelations had come to him, and with predictions of disaster and curses laid upon those who lived drunken and wasteful lives, he urged all men to live morally and to look to the unseen world with gratitude for its blessings. Within ten years Handsome Lake had systematized his teachings with a code of morals and prophecies that he called the *Gaiwiu,* or "Good Message." This was the same term that the Indians applied to the Bible, especially the Gospels; but the Prophet rejected the Bible and argued that his gospel was for Indians and that it was gospel enough. That was too much for Cornplanter, and he broke with his brother on religious issues; he clung to him for political support, however, and they continued their mutual dislike of Red Jacket.

Cornplanter's son Henry recognized the origin of many of Handsome Lake's teachings, and this caused Cornplanter on several occasions to condemn the Prophet. In turn the Prophet condemned Henry along with many other doubters, including Red Jacket. His bitterness caused many Indians in retaliation to call him a deceiver, a fraud.

Chafing under criticism, the time came when Red Jacket openly denounced Handsome Lake as an impostor. A prophet could take care of aspersions like that, and Handsome Lake did so by lashing back at the orator. More and more, as he moved among Indians, urging them to temperance and peaceful pursuits, he heard the echoed scorn of Red Jacket. "Impostor," he heard himself called. But whether charlatan or not, he was doing something for his people that neither teachers nor missionaries had yet done. He had given them new hope, a hope based upon themselves. They had a way of life that was good if they would make the most of themselves. He told them that they need not grovel or lean on alcohol for courage. Hundreds believed him.

Handsome Lake never claimed to be a god, nor did he claim to be perfect in any way. Even though he had many personal faults and had been unfaithful to his duties as a sachem, he had found some inner strength to rise as if from the dead. He believed that a mighty voice speaking from the unseen world of spirits had called upon him to proclaim a new gospel.

Within five years after he had begun his teaching, Handsome Lake had revived the older religion of the Seneca, given it a new force, and produced a sober people. The Quakers were amazed at the result and testified to his success. Even Secretary of War Knox found occasion to praise the Prophet and to give him a passport commending him to all American officials.

The Christian missionaries said that Handsome Lake had created a "new paganism." Even today that accomplishment is a barrier to the religion of the white man, for about twenty per cent of these people still hold to the teachings of the *Gaiwiu* and believe that Handsome Lake was a true prophet.

A non-Christian group led by Red Jacket believed that the Prophet may have started out to reform the old religion but that he had added his own inventions, while condemning some ancient practices believed by many to be good. This branch of objectors claimed that Handsome Lake had changed the old religion and almost destroyed it by altering its character. He had condemned the societies devoted to giving thanks to the birds and animals, for instance. Red Jacket's dilemma, therefore, was to adopt the new paganism, go over to the missionaries, or remain aloof when the Prophet's religious ceremonies were conducted in the long houses.

Handsome Lake continued to have new revelations. He said that, even though his brother Cornplanter had sneered at him, the four angels of the heaven world had restored the latter to favor. Not so, however, with Red Jacket, the villain who had sold all the Indian land and taken all the money for himself.

According to Handsome Lake, he experienced a revelation in which the four messengers appeared and said, "Look! What do you see?"

"I answered that I saw a man carrying dirt in a wheelbarrow. I perceived that he was Red Jacket, a chief, and that his toil must go on forever."

"'Truly spoken,' replied the four messengers. 'It was he who gave consent to the sale of our lands. So you now see the doom of those who repent not. Theirs is an eternity of punishment.'"

Thus did the prophet condemn Red Jacket as a land seller, adroitly blaming him for the acts of others.

Handsome Lake's teachings and revelations created a new reason for religion among the Indians, and the morality that he preached had a deep effect on the behavior of the entire Six Nations, though not all became his followers. Several successors were trained. They memorized the new code. Numbers of his admirers followed him wherever he went, looking upon him as a self-sacrificing hero who was moved only by ideals.

His last journey was to the Onondaga, and among them he died in 1815. Before that he had wandered over the

Allegany reservation, preaching in all the long houses;
he had gone to Cattaraugus settlements and had delivered
his revelations at Tonawanda. His stern call to new duties
and a new dedication separated some families. It was revolting to many, and swung several strong leaders to
Christianity. A choice had to be made.

Red Jacket saw in the *Gaiwiu,* for all its moral teachings,
a reflection of Cornplanter's enmity for him and Handsome Lake's bitterness in general toward those who did
not accept the *Gaiwiu* wholeheartedly. Red Jacket was
placed in an embarrassing position by the Prophet's scorn,
and to this day most Indians of the Six Nations believe that
Red Jacket was actually responsible for the loss of their
ancient lands, a belief not sustained by the facts of history.

[12] *A DECLARATION OF WAR*

IN THE DEEP American wilderness north of Kentucky and
south of the Great Lakes lived many warlike Indian tribes.
Some had settled in fertile places along the rivers, estab-
lishing plantations of corn and beans. Others relied upon
hunting and trade in skins.

Pontiac, the famous leader of the Ottawa tribe, had
tried to teach these people the value of united action. This
thought had been promoted by the British, too. Pontiac's
conspiracy, by which he hoped to expel the whites from the
forts they had built and to capture Detroit, had failed.
By 1806 a new leader of the confederated tribes had arisen

in the person of Tecumseh, an able war captain of the
Shawnee. His spirited orations and appeals to patriotism
made him one of the most admired chiefs of the entire
region west of the Ohio, and most of the western Seneca
as well as the Canadian Mohawk thought him a good man
to follow. Perhaps, they said, he would restore the Indians to their former independence and power. Tecumseh
argued that a new and stronger confederation should be
formed if the white man was to be resisted.

So attractive to venturesome young Seneca warriors was
this plan that many hurried to join Tecumseh's bands and
to lend to him the reputation of their forebears as fighters.
It was thought by some that, if the Indian nations of the
East would support the West, perhaps the Americans
could be kept within due bounds—or perhaps they could
be driven out! It was a forlorn old hope, but Tecumseh
and his fellow chiefs were determined to make the effort.

Knowledge of this plot did not fail to reach Red Jacket,
who deplored that any portion of his people should so
conduct themselves as to endanger all of them and cause
suspicion. With disapproval he heard reports that runners
from the West were continually coming across the Ohio
and the Pennsylvania boundary to hold councils with the
New York Indians. For the Seneca to give any support to
Tecumseh was a violation of the Canandaigua agreement
that peace and friendship should prevail.

Red Jacket knew that he could not honestly conceal this
growing conspiracy of the discontented young Seneca.
He felt that it was his duty to inform Erastus Granger,
federal Indian agent at Buffalo. Red Jacket knew that
young Seneca warriors who supported Tecumseh were not

primarily disloyal but had been carried away by mistaken zeal. He, himself, admired the Shawnee leader and thought of him as one of the greatest Indians who had ever lived, but he knew that he was wrong in his judgment of American power.

When Granger heard Red Jacket's disclosures, he at once became alert. With Red Jacket and his interpreters, Granger took a stagecoach to Washington, the new seat of government. Upon learning of the western plot, the War Department at once became interested, for if the Indians stirred up trouble, the friction already acute with Great Britain would be increased and open, devastating war might follow.

Any resentment that the Six Nations may have harbored would not turn them against the United States if a second war should break out with England, Red Jacket assured the Secretary of War. Twice the Six Nations had sent delegations to the hostile western confederacy, advising the chiefs to refrain from border raids. Red Jacket told the Secretary of War of these honest attempts of his people to keep the peace.

"We have twice sent large delegations to their council fire," he said, "for the purpose of making their minds strong in their friendship with your nation and to urge them, in event of war between the white people, to take no part on either side. As far as our voice has been heard, they agree to listen to our counsel and remain at peace with your nation.

"If war with England should take place, we hope you will inform us through your agents, and we will continue to exert our influence with all the Indians with whom we are acquainted that they . . . cultivate friendship with your people."

One of the things that disturbed Red Jacket was the spell which Elskawatwa, Tecumseh's twin brother, had cast over the hostile tribes. Elskawatwa claimed to be a prophet sent by the Great Spirit to restore all America to the Indians. He promised that warriors who would attack the white men would be free from harm. No bullet could reach them because they would be protected by a magic spell which he would cast over them.

"A war is coming," he predicted, "and you will win it."

The storm of war did break in 1811, but William Henry Harrison, Governor of Indiana, was ready. At the time Tecumseh was away on a southern mission, rousing the drooping spirits of broken tribes and inviting them to join his confederacy. Seizing his opportunity, Elskawatwa lashed his warriors to a frenzy, and under the leadership of warriors White Loon, Stone Eater, and Winemac, an attack was made on white troops at Tippecanoe. Harrison repulsed the onslaught with heavy losses to the Indians. The Shawnee's spell did not work and American bullets struck with fatal results.

More than the frenzied words of Elskawatwa, the encouragement of British officers helped to launch the fatal attack. The Indian losses at Tippecanoe dashed the hopes of Tecumseh and proved that the Americans were not to be caught off guard. The British, too, were disappointed because they hoped to start an Indian war that would keep the Americans too busy to defend themselves when the British invaded the United States along the Atlantic coast and south of the St. Lawrence River.

A little after mid-June, 1812, after much indecision and in the face of strong political opposition in New England and elsewhere, the United States declared war on England. At once British agents appeared among the discontented tribesmen, urging them to take up the hatchet of revenge. Captain Joseph Brant of the Mohawk settlements of Canada, with the rank and pay of a British colonel, sent his emissaries from Canada to the Seneca of New York, urging them to take up arms for the British. Here was the chance at last, he said, for the Seneca and their brothers of the Six Nations to revenge themselves for the frauds suffered from coerced treaties with the Americans. Now, as never before, was the time for the Seneca to reunite with their Canadian Indian kinsmen and fight with honor and profit. Think of what there was to gain!

Red Jacket listened to this invitation with a dark frown. He had never trusted Brant's leanings, and the dislike was mutual. With his accustomed skill as an analyzer of intrigue, he now reasoned the problem pro and con. He was opposed to any move that would seem disloyal to the United States. A promise made by the Six Nations must be kept; Red Jacket would see to it that the promises signed and sealed at Canandaigua were kept.

With this resolution in mind, the leading chiefs of the Seneca sent a delegation to Grand River where the Canadian Mohawk, under Brant, were living. The Mohawk leaders were told in emphatic language that the New York Six Nations were not willing to fight their white neighbors anywhere in the old land of the Iroquois. This meant New York State.

This visit of the Seneca, very likely, was not known to

the whites of Buffalo or the towns near the Niagara River. Not realizing the peaceful intentions of the Seneca, hundreds of residents of western New York feared the revenge of the Indians and began to take measures for protection. All the hatreds of former years were reawakened, and the fear of the Seneca war cry at night filled many a settler with a sleepless dread.

It was then that the agent Erastus Granger called together a council of the New York Indians, some of whom had fought under Elskawatwa in Indiana. When, on July 6, 1812, the council was opened, Red Jacket acted as spokesman. Addressing Granger, he said, "Brother, the voice of war has reached our ears and has made our minds gloomy. We ask you to tell us all the details of the war."

Granger, in reply, explained the causes of the conflict between the Americans and the British. He told how both the British and the French had boarded American ships on the high seas and had seized more than six thousand American sailors. Some of these men the British had forced to fight against American war vessels and other ships. "Now," said Granger, "you have been invited to join with our enemies, the British, in a war against us!" His voice rang out as if to ask, "What are you going to do about it?"

All eyes were upon Red Jacket, who replied for the Six Nations. "My people care more for peace than for war," he said. "Whatever we do, I hope that you will not ask our young men to enter a war the nature of which they cannot understand. The Six Nations are placed in an unpleasant position. A part of our nation lives in Canada and the remainder in the United States. . . . We have lately heard that the Canadian Six Nations have taken up arms.

We are sorry to hear this. They are our blood brothers, and we do not wish their blood to be spilled when there is so little occasion for it."

Though Red Jacket argued for the neutrality of his people, he clearly declared their loyalty to the United States. Referring to the Pickering treaty, he said, "We now declare to you in the presence of all here assembled that we will continue to hold fast to the chain of friendship which unites us."

It is difficult today to realize how much this statement meant to the white people of Buffalo and all western New York. The Seneca were not hostile despite frenzied rumors, and this evident fact made a deep impression. It became the occasion for the printing of the first book published in Buffalo. The volume, which contained the complete texts of both Granger's and Red Jacket's speeches, was read with avid interest by the relieved citizens of New York from the Hudson River to Chautauqua Lake.

Yet the Seneca people eventually did go to war. As they traveled from their little hamlets to the teeming town at the mouth of Buffalo Creek, they saw hundreds of white men in new uniforms, heard the strains of martial music, watched the parades, and listened to the huzzas of volunteers. Such displays of military might deeply stirred the Indians. But even the glitter of arms had its lesson; it recalled the miseries that followed Sullivan's terrible raid, and this made the leaders of the Six Nations value peace.

Then something happened that jarred their neutrality. British troops had crossed the Niagara and had seized Grand Island, which was Seneca territory!

Because the Seneca regarded themselves as an independent nation, they regarded this invasion as an act of war. War had again come to them—the Seneca! There was no question now about what must be done. Red Jacket immediately called a council to which agent Granger was also bidden. Conditions had changed and must be understood and discussed. No longer did this new war concern only American sailors far out in the eastern ocean.

To Granger, Red Jacket said, "Brother, you have told us that we have nothing to do with the war that has taken place between you and the British. But now we find that war has come to our own door. Our property is taken possession of by the British and their Indian friends. It is now necessary for us to defend our property and drive the enemy from it. If we sit still and take no redress, the British according to the customs of you white people will hold Grand Island by conquest. And should you conquer the Canadas, you will claim it upon the same principles, as though you had conquered it from the British. We, therefore, ask permission to go with our warriors and drive off those bad people and repossess our lands."

The agent had no objections to offer, and this was the signal to go ahead. From the council house at Buffalo Creek, an invitation was dispatched by runners, and from every corner of the Six Nations world, save Canada, came eager tribesmen. All were incensed at the news of invasion. The council that followed, one of the largest ever held to discuss the welfare of the Six Nations, resulted in a formal declaration of war against Great Britain.

The Six Nations and their six hundred warriors were arrayed against all Canada and with it the whole British Empire. The American commander on the Niagara fron-

tier was not yet ready to accept Indian volunteers, but he
did challenge the white population to enlist by declaring,
"Even the Indians of the friendly Six Nations have offered
their services, but through regard to the cause of humanity, I have refused to follow a disgraceful example by
letting loose these barbarous warriors upon the inhabitants
of Canada."

With far greater realism the Canadians had accepted the
aid of their own Six Nations allies and their associates in
the West. They were in the war as soon as they could be
equipped.

Since the war was not going as well as hoped, the Seneca
soon learned that the Americans had changed their minds
about allowing Indians to fight. Now Indians were ur-
gently wanted. American agents were scouring the reservations, offering inducements and commissions. Young
Henry O'Bail was made a major of infantry and given
command of the Allegany Seneca. So serious was the need
for men, now that the Niagara shore of New York had
been threatened with invasion, that two hundred Indians
living nearby were enlisted. In every Indian village, war
clubs and other traditional weapons were whittled out and
polished, and old guns were found and repaired. It was
some time, however, before each Indian recruit had a good
gun and sufficient ammunition.

Fortified by their own resolution to fight and armed
with guns and cutlasses, the Indians of the Six Nations
army were allied to the American army. A sharp engagement near Squaw Island in the Niagara River soon tested
their mettle and proved the trust placed in them. Reporting
on their military conduct, the American commander, Gen-

eral Porter, wrote, "They committed no act of cruelty, and although some of them proposed after the skirmish to scalp the slain according to their ancient customs, they evinced no displeasure when sharply refused."

For all his influence with his people, Red Jacket seems to have been given only the rank of captain. He was sixty-two years old but a supple and alert man. His courage and leadership were tested in the successful attack on Fort George, July 17, 1813, when he led a surprise attack on British and Indian troops stationed there.

As the war continued along both sides of the Niagara, the American Six Nations were found in nearly every major battle. Their devotion even brought about the enlistment of six Oneida women, who shouldered guns and fought at the side of their husbands.

That Indians of the Six Nations on both sides of the Canadian border should be fighting each other face to face made Red Jacket and some of the older chiefs feel that the better contribution to the war would be to bring about the withdrawal of their Canadian brethren. Accordingly, Red Jacket dispatched two young scouts to the British lines, ordering them to pass through the battle front and reach the Mohawk troops. This was done and a mutual withdrawal from the war was proposed. The scouts succeeded, and within a short time each body of Indian warriors returned to their respective reservations. Some, however, enlisted in the regular army and fought on to the end.

In every engagement up to the time of the withdrawal, Red Jacket had shown valor as a soldier, facing the enemy without apparent fear as he led his troops forward. Only Cornplanter ever accused him of cowardice. Other responsible Indian officers made no such charge, and we may assume that the smear was but one of the episodes in a long feud between men who had no love for each other.

In 1815 peace between the British and Americans had been restored, and the Six Nations relaxed their tension. Transforming changes had come over them, especially the Seneca. War had not been without its benefits by way of discipline and a new comradeship between the Indians and the whites. Some continued their friendly relations as long as they lived.

[13] *IT SHALL BE LIKE A ROCK*

As THE RUMBLINGS of the War of 1812 died down, six hundred soldiers of the Six Nations, finding themselves veterans of a conflict that was not of their making, began to examine their own situation. Their chiefs were still worried because of the unsettled question of the ownership of the land they occupied. Did they or did they not have a right to live upon it, or had some other right fallen over it like a net?

Some of the chiefs who had mingled with the neighboring whites thought that the old claims of Massachusetts still held, though they did not agree that these claims were logical or right. But right had been determined by law, even though they had no part in making the law. Another factor, which they did not like to admit, was that as British allies in the Revolution they had been defeated. The stinging words of General Butler at Fort Stanwix still rankled. "You are a conquered people!" he had declared to the Indians.

Their most able interpreters, like Horatio Jones and Jasper Parrish, whom they highly regarded, explained the American government's position without mincing words: "They [the Americans] say we were whipped when the British quit. That being so, we are here only because Washington . . . said we could stay. We are here subject to what their own laws say about it, and they say the claims of the land companies are good. They can buy us out at their own price."

"Maybe," answered Red Jacket, his face very grave. "Maybe! But I never heard that we had any land we wanted to sell."

"No land!" exclaimed Jones. "Well, it is true you never offered any for sale."

And it is certainly true that neither the Seneca nor any of their kindred ever walked into a land office or government department and used any words that could be faintly construed as an offer to sell an acre of land.

By the time the War of 1812 had ended, the Holland Land Company had disposed of most of its holdings west of the Genesee. To Colonel Aaron Ogden and his associates had been sold the right to treat with the Seneca Indians and their allies for the land which the Indians still owned after the sale to Morris.

The time was rapidly approaching when the Ogdens could apply a well-nigh irresistible pressure upon the Seneca and by one device or another induce them to release what they loved most. Added to dishonest arguments and a hypocritical concern for the welfare of the Seneca was the fact that Ogden had a strong political position. What were nonvoting Indians in the face of this power? What chance did the Indians have in view of the common belief that the Indians would be better off if they were to move to a far-western region? By doing so, they would escape the evils of white communities. Certain white leaders as well as Red Jacket and other responsible Indians knew that Ogden's real purpose, however, was to buy the lands for as little as possible and sell them at large profits to the hordes of settlers who were demanding homesteads and fertile acres.

Nevertheless, Joseph Brant listened to the arguments of the land company and became convinced that it might be a good idea to have the Seneca move to Sandusky, Ohio, where they could join with the Wyandot Indians. The Wyandot spoke a language much like the Seneca. He went to Buffalo Creek to place the plan before the Seneca. Of course this played directly into the hands of the Ogden interests, but it is not believed that Brant had been bribed. He had another motive, that of luring the Seneca into a league with several western tribes. This league would be controlled by the British, and Brant, as a British officer, could become the head of a buffer state of strongly armed

Indians. Brant did not mention this to the Seneca. "Let us form a grand council," he said. "We can forget our troubles and become a military power once more. In the West the white men cannot oppress us, and we shall be free."

We do not know what Red Jacket said to this appeal, though many Seneca approved it. To him the very proposal obscured the more important problem of holding on to the lands the Seneca still possessed in New York. Brant's eloquence made Red Jacket suspect that he had a malign political motive. However, since a council was to be held in any event, Red Jacket with his friends George Hosmer and Jasper Parrish undertook the journey. With them were numerous Seneca warriors, eager to observe the action of the western tribes.

Upon the arrival of the Seneca, the council was called to order and speeches of welcome by several chiefs of western tribes were made. The chiefs of the Six Nations, long accustomed to the clothing of the white man, were once more dressed in their ancient costumes. The western leaders looked at them and wondered if, after all, these eastern chiefs, with their close knowledge of the white man's ways, were not the very strength that was needed for a successful revolt against the Americans.

On the morning of November 7, 1816, Red Jacket stepped to the council fire of the assembled tribes. Every eye was fixed upon the fiery orator whose fame as an opponent of the sale of Indian land was known far and wide. Though he opposed the settlers, he was equally insistent that the Indians get along peaceably with them. What now would he say when still ringing in his ears were the angry

words of the western chiefs who had expressed the hope
that by force of arms the settlers who refused to obey
treaties or government orders might be frightened back
by a bloody war.

Red Jacket, his face filled with pity, looked at his audience and slowly said, "We have been here before to
offer advice." He reminded the leaders of the western tribes
that the advice of the Six Nations had not been accepted in
1794; as a result Wayne had won a victory that cost hundreds of Indian lives. He reminded them of the council
held with Tecumseh, Blue Coat, and Elskawatwa, in which
Six Nations leaders advised a settlement of disputes with
the American government to be arrived at by reason rather
than guns. If there were to be a war between Great
Britain and the United States, we advised Indians to be
neutral, he said. "You didn't believe us. What followed?
You lost your greatest leader and hundreds of warriors
you could ill spare, because you thought Great Britain
would whip the Americans and regain for you your lost
lands."

He reminded the Shawnee, Ottawa, and Wyandot chiefs,
especially, that wars with the whites always left the Indians poorer, weaker in manpower, and pressed by the
victorious whites to sell more of their land as a price of
peace. "We have always lost by taking up the hatchet,"
he exclaimed. "Even the British, upon whom we pinned
our hopes, sold our land to the Americans after every war
in which we were allied with them."

War might come again, he said, and if it did, the western
Indians would be invited by the British to join them once

more. "If we listen to their counsel, we shall be extermi-
nated. Let us guard against this by forming a permanent
union that shall protect us in the future."

The union of which Red Jacket here was thinking was
a revival of the old Iroquois league of the Six Nations, a
union of people whose moral strength would be united in
an unmovable resolution to accept what had happened but
to sell no more land. It was to be a league of peace.

"Do not be flattered by any white people who may wish
to purchase your land," he shouted. "To command respect,
you must possess extensive territory! Keep your holdings
sufficiently large so that you may not be crowded on any
side by the whites."

Not a few of the Wyandot had been in New York, and
they knew, as Brant knew, that the land of the Six Nations
was now small indeed.

"You were the first to give away your lands," answered
a western leader. "These lands were regions on which you
ought to have reared your women and children." The
reference, of course, was to the land sales at Big Tree in
1797.

The leaders of the Six Nations looked as if they had been
slapped.

"You advise us to take good care of our lands," went on
the speaker. "We thank you for that counsel and are very
sorry that you did not take better care of yours. We now
give you the same advice. Take care of your land. We
shall take good care of ours. We have not much left!"

Red Jacket smiled, for he had extracted from his allies
the very message that he wanted to have his own people
receive. He had turned the council designed to stir up

more hatred against the whites into a consideration of getting along with the whites, and he had emphasized the importance of holding on to the lands that remained as their own.

This long council at Sandusky was not attended by any government officer. The only record of what was said was made by George Hosmer, Red Jacket's white friend. The bare record is important, however, since it shows the determination of the Six Nations that they would never again take up arms against their white neighbors whatever the provocation might be.

Red Jacket hated war and bloodshed, though he had been a warrior. Even in battle he had been kind and humane. He had never taken a scalp, though the British were paying handsomely for them. When some jesting warriors had noticed Red Jacket's squeamishness, they handed him a dripping scalp.

"Here," said a sneering warrior. "Take this and you can have at least one to boast about."

"Poor fool!" exclaimed Red Jacket, stalking away in disgust.

When Red Jacket returned from Sandusky, he became even more impressed with the weakness of the position of his people. The surging race of white men was too great for them to resist by force. He had seen the little band of six hundred in the War of 1812 and the thousands of white soldiers, who were but a token of the tens of thousands more that might be mustered. Resistance was hopeless unless, as Young King had said, the Seneca learned all that the white man knew. To Red Jacket it was unthinkable that this learning could be achieved in schools. He did not understand and did not like the young Indian men who returned from schools only to lapse into discontent and idleness. He did not understand even those who stayed with the whites and took up their positions as white men. There was Jacob Jemison, the surgeon, who dressed like a white doctor and wanted to talk English. It seemed a denial of everything that was old and sacred.

"We must learn by watching," he told Little Beard (son of the elder chief), who now was at Tonawanda. "We must keep ourselves separate and live as our fathers, changing only to accommodate our living on our smaller lands."

"We can no longer live as our fathers," put in Young King. "Times have changed." He pointed to Little Beard and asked, "The school at Tonawanda has not hurt our Indians, has it?"

"The school will help us know what the white man says when he comes to buy our lands," answered Little Beard. "Jemmy Johnson and Blacksmith say the teacher is good," he added.

"Remember," said Red Jacket with a scowl, "if we become like the white man and learn the white man's stories, we shall think as the white man and then sell more of our lands. I say again, hold on to your land at Tonawanda, hold on at Buffalo, hold on along the Genesee!"

It was certainly true that the lands remaining to the Seneca were situated in fertile spots, that they were broad and well drained, that they were ample to support life. Along the Genesee there still remained the reserved lands about the villages of Big Tree, Caneadea, Canawaugus,

Beardstown, and Gardeau. Greater areas spread out along the valleys of Tonawanda, Buffalo Creek, and the long vale of the Allegheny where it arched into New York and went out again.

Over all this forested territory, over every stream and waterfall, over the cleared lands where the Seneca had hopefully built new homes, there hovered the dark cloud of the Ogden right to buy when the Indians agreed. The landed interests now began to make this right effective by pulling political strings.

In the summer of 1819 the Ogden company, by arrangement with the government, invited the Seneca to a council at Buffalo Creek. To watch out for the best interests of the Indians, Judge Morris Miller, of Oneida County, was appointed federal commissioner, while Nathaniel Gorham represented Massachusetts. These watchful agents were to see that the Indians were not cheated or deceived by false statements.

After preliminary pleasantries, Ogden frankly stated his purpose. "I will buy your reservation for good money," he told the chiefs. "You are at disadvantage here at Buffalo with white people all about you. Sell and let everybody go to the Allegany reservation, there to be together instead of scattered."

Red Jacket's eyes were blazing. But his brother chiefs sat silently meditating. They knew that it was futile to object. The old fight in their souls was gone, and a yielding attitude prevailed. Little Billy, Tall Chief, Young King, Two Skies, Infant, and Destroy Town were silent as the Ogden agents presented their argument—all couched in glowing terms to show that the Seneca would be benefited by the offer.

All the Genesee River settlements were described as far out of the way, surrounded by settlers, inconvenient, and of little value to the Indians. Now came the bald proposal that these be given up—that Buffalo Creek be given up.

Judge Miller, to aid the land buyers but ostensibly to soothe the fears of the Indians, arose to explain that the Great White Father, the President of the United States, had considered the welfare of his red children and wished "to extend to them security and the useful arts." To have the benefit of security, the Seneca now "should concentrate upon the land reservation on the Allegheny, the title to which should be ceded to them in fee, as the white man holds his lands." Or, if they wished, they might have liberty to join their brothers at Sandusky, Ohio. If they did this, they would get full price for their New York lands and get the western lands free.

"Ah," exclaimed the fatherly protector of Indian rights sent by the government. "Good men might advise you to hold your lands, as, no doubt, the Quakers did, but bad whites also must be reckoned with." These, he explained, must be avoided, and to do that, it was best to move away.

To a large body of friendly Indians and to the sympathetic whites of the region, these fatherly words, emanating from President Monroe's easy chair, seemed benevolent and thoughtful of the red man's truest interests (not to speak of the financial interests of the obliging Ogden company).

Red Jacket, who inwardly was seething at the insult offered to the intelligence of any informed man, kept his anger in check. In response to Judge Miller he said, "The commissioner told us of his own 'care' for his red children, but is now inviting us to sell cheaply, a strange way to protect us." However, he did invite a frank discussion and promised an answer to the main question—removal to the Ohio country.

To this unexpectedly mild speech, David A. Ogden, of the company, replied, giving his version of what the company's rights were and the early relations of New York and Massachusetts that had brought about the right. It was the old story, the sophistries of which were always the occasion of astonishment to the Seneca even though they had heard them related many times. Holding his anger in check, Red Jacket began to discuss the several treaties by which Seneca lands had been absorbed. Of these agreements, he said, "We too understand them. When we made a treaty with Colonel Pickering, we were told that it was to be permanent and lasting between us and the United States forever." He looked at the Ogden agents and eyed Judge Miller accusingly.

"Even before that," he went on to say as he ran his hand over the Washington medal he wore, "there was a meeting in Philadelphia to which the Six Nations had been invited. An agreement was reached, and General Washington declared that it should be permanent between the red and the white brothers, that it would be spread out on the largest and strongest rocks that nothing could undermine or break, that it should be exposed to the view of all."

Then he confessed that even then he had been fearful, and "I told our white brothers that I feared eventually they would wish to disturb those contracts. You white brothers," he exploded, "have the faculty to burst the stoutest of rocks. On our part we have not disturbed a single treaty."

With the present "disturbance" in mind, he paused to look at Judge Miller and then slowly said, "We do not understand why the treaty made by one [President] is not binding on the other."

Thoroughly aroused now, still leading up to the proposal of the Ogdens that the land should be sold, he no longer restrained his anger. "This is our land from Heaven," he shouted. "We cannot make land. Driven back and reduced as we are, you wish to cramp us still more. You speak of 'pre-emptive right,' indeed. Such men as you say you should have this reservation, and others say take another. But they [these reservations] are all ours from the top to the bottom!"

His anger was growing, and he raised his voice again. "You say the lands are yours. Only if I should see Mr. Ogden coming down from Heaven to say that the Heavenly Father had bestowed the title, would I believe him. The President must have had a distorted mind when he offered to lead us by the arm to the Allegany reservation."

He referred to the swampy edges of the streams and the unproductive and uninhabitable mountain spurs, but his voice was still vibrating with rage as he closed his address by shouting, "We will not part with any of our reservations. Do not make your application anew nor in any other shape. Let us hear no more of it." With this the council of 1819 adjourned.

Though the subject was dismissed at the first Buffalo council, it arose at other councils that were held in 1822 and 1823. Every persuasion was used, but Red Jacket remained adamant, his logic cutting through falsehood and connivance.

Finally the aging chief, wearied by his long efforts, withdrew. Shortly afterward, by means of costly gifts and life pensions, the majority of chiefs were persuaded to sign a release to the Genesee lands. "It is not to be escaped," they said. "They are right, and they would have had these lands anyway. It is of no use to resist."

"You need not sign," the federal agent told Red Jacket. But knowing that he was required to do so if the majority had signed, the chief made the matter unanimous, as required by Seneca law. His mark is to be found on the agreement.

Thus were liquidated the pleasant little Indian settlements along the Genesee, and larger reservations were reduced by many thousand acres. For the 87,526 acres so released, the sum of fifty-five cents an acre was paid. The land was quickly sold for twenty to sixty times that amount. Federal commissioners, delegated to prevent "cheating of the Indians," entirely forgot that they might have insisted upon a much higher compensation at a public sale, the profits of which could have been used to benefit these Indians for many years. As it was, the scale of fortune was tipped for the profit of the land company, and for over a century the taxpayers of New York State and of the United States have been paying out of their pockets thousands of dollars to make up the oversight. Roads, schools, health supervision, welfare, and police protection might have been paid for out of the Indians' own funds with a large measure of self-respect. It would have been their money and not the taxpayers'.

As it is, many descendants of these same people now feel that nothing the state or the nation can do is too much; anything spent is only conscience money, and they take it as partial restitution.

But even conscience money may have a good effect. Red Jacket lived to see this when more and more of his young people were given training and education. In this way they were becoming interwoven in the common fabric of society that makes a nation of many people one in purpose.

The eternal "rock of agreement" upon which the Seneca relied when they talked with George Washington has undergone many changes. The Indians and the whites have changed as well, and now this rock has become a part of the foundation that upholds the structure of a government in which the Seneca and their brethren may participate as citizens and voters. The promised anchorage indeed has been "like a rock."

[14] *IT ALL ENDED*
WITH A CHERRY TABLE

THE LITTLE VILLAGES along Buffalo Creek in 1820 were different from those of a century and a half earlier. The earlier, enormous bark lodges had disappeared. In their places were individual cabins, some of logs and some of planks, but nearly all were covered with roofs of sheet bark.

Red Jacket's house was of logs and not very large. It sat in the open along the reservation road and was near the two-story frame building occupied by interpreter William Jones. The two were bosom friends and were often invited to the better homes of Buffalo—homes of men who thought of themselves as philosophers, liberals, and free-thinkers. In such company the astute chief picked up a vast amount of information. Some of the whites he met were critical of their own race, and were said by certain people of Buffalo to have encouraged Red Jacket in some of his sharpest arguments against the white man's civilization.

Fortified with facts and prejudices, the aging chief often astonished his acquaintances with his knowledge of men and events.

Descendants of Red Jacket's neighbors a half century after his death often talked of his ability as a conversationist, recalling traditions of his many visits at Tonawanda and Buffalo Creek villages. Aurelia Jones, granddaughter of the interpreter, used to tell her friends how the old chief would sit during conversation as if he heard nothing at all and then spring to his feet and sweep away arguments by uttering a few pointed words. He was a welcome visitor in many circles, but he frequently would upset a whole evening's deliberation by showing how faulty the conclusions of the speakers were. This sometimes pricked the pride of Indian leaders, more and more of whom secretly envied and hated him.

In the little Indian towns, with their open fields where games were played, Chief Jacket was a familiar figure. He was a great favorite with the women, often doing errands for them or acting as their spokesman in their frequent councils. He had a bantering way with the children and was gracious to their mothers. The more dignified chiefs, like Young King and Captain Pollard, thought him too familiar and resented his easy manner with the villagers.

At home he was a quiet man, tending his garden thoughtfully but more often sitting on the ground pondering a speech that he was preparing for the next council. Usually he dressed with great neatness, smoothing his woolen outer garments and dressing his hair with care. Often he wore his red coat with gilt epaulets, but sometimes he would rise in the late morning, go outside, and bask in his night clothing to the distress of Mrs. Jacket.

It is quite probable that he irritated all three of his wives, one of whom died, one of whom he divorced, and the third, Degeney. There is little in tradition about his first wife, Wyashoh. Inquiry at the Cattaraugus reservation some fifty years ago indicated that she died of tuberculosis and that all his children perished of the same malady. His next venture into matrimony was with a beautiful young woman who could not endure his silent habits and lack of attention. She left him to find happier surroundings and did not lack for sympathy or male admirers. Red Jacket mourned for a while. He then visited her, asking for a reconciliation, but was repulsed.

After a number of years, about 1820 he took for his wife the widow Two Guns, whose children he also loved. She was a bright, intelligent woman of nearly fifty years who had survived the terrors of the Revolution, in which so many of her people had perished. Keeping house for a public figure was no easy task, even though her husband was a good provider and kind to her children. She had few callers in the new location, for her friends and neighbors lived in widely spaced cabins with individual gardens. This was far different from the old days when ten or more women lived in a long house and worked their large fields together. Although few such houses were still in existence at this time, Mrs. Jacket had lived in one during her earlier years.

One day the missionary dropped in and invited her to come to the new church where wonderful stories were told. "You will be welcome," he said, smiling and speaking in the Seneca tongue. "My name is Harris, Thompson Harris; you must have heard your husband speak of me."

Mrs. Jacket shrank back in a dark corner. Plainly she was filled with terror. "Oh, if I dared come," she replied in a sad voice.

"You need not be afraid," answered the missionary. "A Power greater than that of any man will care for you."

"My children have told me about you," she said. "They believe in you, but Jacket says you have come to steal our land."

"That cannot be true, for even Red Jacket cannot point out a single acre that we have asked for or that we own."

"He says your church and your house are on our land and you will take more land."

"It is not our house," replied Mr. Harris. "It belongs to the Power I spoke about."

"Oh, if I only dared!" she exclaimed.

"Don't be afraid," said the missionary. "Come!"

Encouraged to do so by her children, Ruth and Daniel Two Guns, Degeney did go to church, and despite her irate husband she stole away to the mission every Sunday morning thereafter. There she heard in her own language a message that stirred her deeply. Week after week she listened and learned to sing hymns that gave her a deeper faith.

After services one Sunday she told Mr. Harris of her desire to become one of his flock. Mrs. Harris took her aside to instruct her in what this meant.

"I have done bad things, and I'm sorry," she told Mrs. Harris. "Could I have these things forgotten?"

"Just listen to the wonderful story," counseled the good lady. "All you need to do is ask, and your burden will fall away."

After a period of trial, Mrs. Jacket was received into the Seneca Mission Church, and there she found herself with staunch friends. The elderly John Pollard and his wife were members; so were Seneca White and Young King and their wives. Mrs. Jacket became the thirty-seventh communicant, and six others confessed their faith on the same day.

When, some time later, Red Jacket as leader of the Anti-Christian party learned of his wife's action, he was thoroughly angry. It placed his household under direct missionary influence and under the influence of Pollard, leader of the new party—the Christian party. This was too much!

"Give up that church!" commanded Red Jacket. "Leave those grasping people! They have come to deceive us and make a path for land-grabbers."

"I cannot give up my belief."

"If you do not quit all contact with missionaries, I will leave you, and when I do, I will have them driven out—— out!" The chief was fuming.

Mrs. Jacket held her ground. It was her house. She

would not abandon it or her new association. The lives she saw were clean; the lives of the converts were transformed. Both the men and the women had a new incentive to be honest and industrious.

"I wanted to be a Christian a long time," she told Mrs. Harris. "A long time ago I wanted to join the church, but I was afraid of my famous husband."

"There is a more noble fame," Mrs. Harris had told her. "Fear not, God is with you."

After frowning and refraining from speaking for a few days, Red Jacket disappeared. He was reported to have left for Tonawanda, where he had relatives and clansmen—staunch old-timers, he thought.

He turned up at the cabin of the son of Little Beard and announced that he had changed his residence and told why. Beard was quite astonished and sent him to Tonawanda Falls, where Dragon Fly and his hospitable wife of the Wolf clan lived in a large log house. There Red Jacket had often stayed before, and now it would be a place where he might see old friends.

Dragon Fly's home was, indeed, a meeting place for many white visitors and tribal chiefs. It was situated along the creek trail over which most travelers came from the East. Here everyone was welcome and could get a meal and enjoy Seneca hospitality.

Without immediate explanation, the tired and bewildered Red Jacket entered Dragon Fly's house and took his old seat by the window. Greeted cordially, he was offered a bowl of corn soup, which he eagerly ate. That night he slept beneath clean blankets in a bunk near the door. Next morning he slowly walked down to the falls and sat looking at the tumbling water. How like a little Niagara it was.

It was several months before he mustered courage to speak to his clan relative Mrs. Dragon Fly about his problem.

"I've left my wife," he announced. "She has become a Christian."

"She is a good woman," replied Mrs. Dragon Fly.

"She is a friend of the missionaries now," said Red Jacket. "I do not like this because Pollard will laugh at me and say, 'See, even your woman has given up the old religion.' That was the old way of our fathers, and I am hurt that she should turn her back on me and forget old things."

"She is a good woman," repeated Mrs. Dragon Fly, glancing at her husband.

"But she is a Christian now!"

"So am I," replied Mrs. Dragon Fly.

"You!"

"Yes, and so is Dragon Fly!"

Red Jacket sprang up, shouting, "No, that cannot be so! You, Dragon Fly, were with me in the war; you never went to see the chaplain. We were at Chippewa, Fort George, Black Rock—remember? I knew that you were of the old faith of our fathers."

"I am a Christian now," replied Dragon Fly. "Some of our best men have changed their minds about the old ways. We have found out that not many of our white neighbors are bad men. Bad men are not Christians."

"But you are Seneca," argued Red Jacket. "How can you take upon yourselves the religion of the white people?"

"Because," replied Dragon Fly, "it tells us that we are not only Seneca but also brothers of the white man and that we can sing and pray together. We are mankind now, not only Seneca. Christians believe in always being kind to each other."

In his halting way, Dragon Fly told the story of his great decision and how the new religion made men wish to love their neighbors and not harm them. "Don't you see?" he asked. "The missionaries live only to do good to others, not themselves. They never ask one thing for themselves."

"Still I don't trust them," frowned Red Jacket.

"Then who else gives us schools, brings us medicine, wants us to be happy, all without asking payment?"

"They will ask for it by and by. You watch!"

"I'll watch," said Dragon Fly.

"Yes, watch and see the land-grabbers come. Then the missionaries will tell you to sign a treaty."

"Preachers never asked us to sign any treaty. They didn't like the land companies any more than we did. But we took the presents, drank the rum, and then took the pen and made our marks on the agreements."

"Listen to me," commanded Red Jacket. "The time will come when, because you are the brothers of Christians, the land-grabbers will come to Tonawanda. They will smile and try to make you sign and sell. You Tonawanda people are the last strong rock of our nation, and if you give up, our people are lost!"

"We will never give up, and we shall never sign another treaty!" said Dragon Fly firmly.

"If I could only believe you," said Red Jacket, and his eyes were filled with tears.

"You can believe me," replied Dragon Fly. "We shall never sign another paper."

"Good. But tomorrow I speak in the long house, and I want you to hear me. I shall advise the people against becoming Christians and against selling more land."

Red Jacket did speak in the long house, and the Tonawanda for many long years remembered his words. Twelve years later they lost their reservation to the land company as Red Jacket had predicted. The name of every Tonawanda chief was found upon the document, but every name, as shown by sworn statements submitted to Congress, was proved to be a forgery. Yet the "treaty" was ratified by the United States Senate by a majority of one.

After his speech of warning, Red Jacket went back to his seat at the side of the falls. He felt that his work was almost over, and he was exhausted. He was becoming lonely for his cabin at Buffalo Creek. He missed the children. Did they miss him? He returned to Dragon Fly's house, where he lifted an infant from its cradle. "What's his name?" he asked.

"His Indian name is Name Leader," replied his mother, "but we are going to call him Ely as his Christian name."

"And this boy?" he grasped an older child and placed him on his knee.

"That one is Good Voice," said the mother, "but we call him Nicholson, and Dragon Fly has been christened William."

"White-man names!" exclaimed Red Jacket. "Keep the old names!"

As he sat in a new chair in Dragon Fly's home, he remarked that the family was "almost white folk now. See, you have a table!"

"William made the table," said Mrs. Dragon Fly. "You go back home and make a table for Mrs. Jacket. She will like it."

After much meditation and some mumbling to himself, the aging chief announced his departure. "I shall go home," he said. "I shall try to feel at home with a Christian woman."

"That won't hurt you," smiled Mrs. Dragon Fly. "Show her that, even if you follow the old way, you can be kind. Remember she didn't drive you out!"

Return he did, and his homecoming was somewhat awkward. When his wife saw him, fearing that he might be in an angry mood, she ran to a neighbor's house. But the children rushed out to meet him and placed their arms about his neck, kissing him again and again. He went inside and his wife, recovering from her misgivings, came in. She greeted him cheerfully as if he had not been away.

"There's news," she said finally. "The teacher, James Young, is going to print a book for us to read. The missionary is going to print songs so that we can sing—in our own language!"

Red Jacket groaned. "What news!" he mumbled. "Books for Indians! Books were not meant for us."

Glad, nevertheless, to be home once more, Red Jacket did everything he could to atone for his absence. Degeney and the children tried to satisfy his every whim, and he seemed to enjoy himself as never before. Little Ruth greeted him every morning and braided his thinning hair. He would kiss her cheek and pat her head.

On one occasion a meal had been prepared and placed, ready to eat, on a deerskin outside the door. Soon the rattle of carriages was heard, and Mrs. Jacket, ashamed of her primitive way of serving food, fled indoors.

"They are coming," she whispered. "Sightseers are coming here!" She beckoned to her children to come inside. "They will make fun of us," she said. "They will say we eat on the ground like animals."

"Stay where you are," commanded Red Jacket. "These white people sometimes eat; there is nothing strange about eating."

The carriages stopped, and several men and women walked up to the cabin. Red Jacket was clothed only in his long nightshirt and moccasins, not having taken time to dress. He arose from the grass with the utmost dignity and saluted the sightseers, shook hands, and invited them to sit down with him.

Mrs. Jacket was greatly embarrassed, thinking her family had been disgraced, but her husband never so much as considered his bedroom attire. After the visitors had had their view and had gone away, he heard his wife's sobs and sensed her humiliation. He was not long in seeking to cure it.

A few days later he was seen struggling over the trail with something enormous and clumsy strapped to his back.

Reaching home, to his wife's amazement and delight, he brought in a new, drop-leaf, cherry table, the best he could buy in Buffalo.

"Here, Mother," he said. "Here is a table like Mrs. Dragon Fly's at Tonawanda. Now we can eat like white folk. I'll get you some dishes, too!"

Mother Jacket, her eyes filling with tears, could hardly speak. Red Jacket saw her pleasure and felt better himself, though lugging a table for five miles had been something of a task.

Sixty-three years later Ruth Two Gun Stevenson, the little child who had done his braids, used the table in her own dining room. Both her mother and stepfather long had gone to their rest. She often told the story of the table to people who came to see her at her flourishing farm near Irving, New York, where "white folk" were proud to dine with her and her Mose.

Needless to say, the Stevenson home was a neat and well-furnished one. Ruth Stevenson had many callers, among them historians and writers who wanted to know about her honored stepfather. From her they learned much about Red Jacket's later life.

Proudly she would serve her friends the delicacies she knew how to prepare on the cherry table that had signaled Red Jacket's change of heart. For a long time the unlearned Seneca thought that the missionary's word "charitable" meant to atone for misdeeds by doing what Red Jacket had done. It was being "cherry table"!

[15] *HIS WORDS*
WERE AS THE LIGHTNING

WHEN RED JACKET stepped into a room, he attracted immediate attention, for his whole body seemed to radiate an electric presence. He was above medium height and graceful. His expressive face made him stand out from all others. It was not stolid or inscrutable, like the faces of so many of his people, but lively. His eyes, for example, when he was talking or even listening, glowed with a hidden fire that actually seemed to blaze. Often he smiled so broadly that someone would ask him what the joke was. Then he would utter a sentence that summed up a whole discussion, and everybody would laugh. Indians were great laughers, and their jokes were sometimes full of sly wisdom.

All those who were within range of Red Jacket's voice, it is said, felt its magic, though, in the case of the whites, not a word could be understood. When he spoke, his very tones, his gestures, and his pauses conveyed the vigor of his words. His voice was vibrant, modulated, and rhythmic and flowed with a cadence that held his listeners spellbound.

He almost always spoke in his native tongue, usually refraining from any attempt to use his halting English. This, however, was a risk that he had to take, for every interpreter admitted that an exact translation was impossible. Not one of them was able to convey in English the intricate weaving of his metaphors or to imitate his measured sentences. All these qualities made him a welcome guest, and numerous distinguished persons made an effort to meet him at the home of some friend who knew him well.

In 1824 Dr. John Breckenridge met the orator at a dinner. Later, the doctor in his record described the occasion:

Red Jacket was in appearance nearly sixty years [he was actually seventy-four] at this time. He had a weather-beaten look; age had done something to produce this—probably intemperance more. But still his general appearance was strictly kind and his face noble. His lofty and capacious forehead, his piercing black eye, his gently curved lips, fine cheek and slightly aquiline nose, all marked the great man, and, as sustained and expressed by his dignified air, made a deep impression on everyone who saw him. All these features became doubly impressive when his mind and body were set in motion by the effort of speaking—if effort that may be called which flowed like a free, full stream from his lips. I saw him in the wane of life and heard him only in private, and through a stupid and careless interpreter. Yet notwithstanding all these disadvantages he was one of the greatest men and most eloquent orators I ever knew.

Those who understood only English naturally could not appreciate all that Red Jacket said even when translated. Some of the interpreters were uneducated men who were unable to translate the beauty of the orator's language. This is why interpretations were often a disappointment after hearing the even and rhythmic flow of his words. His emphatic tones, gestures, facial expressions, and the flashing of his eyes plainly had meaning that did not find explanation in the English of the interpreter. Many warm friends of the chief wrote about this quality of his speeches and said that, though a white audience could not understand his words, it enjoyed listening to him. It was like hearing the poetry of a great song from the throat of a master singer.

Sometimes, however, he laid aside his dignity and jokingly made a pun in English. Some of his puns continued to be told for many years after his death. For example, when a missionary named Cram preached too long in the council house, Red Jacket observed, "It appears that he is trying to cram his ideas down our throats!"

The orator was sometimes not above sarcasm and occasionally used it to drive home a point. While attending a trial in Batavia, New York, he heard to his amazement that a man had been given a life sentence for stealing a horse. On leaving the courthouse with a lawyer friend, Red Jacket looked up at the coat of arms of the State of New

York, pointing first to the figure on the left side of the shield. His interpreter crudely but effectively translated his questions.

"Who him?"

"That is the figure of Liberty," he was told.

"So it is; well, who him call?" He pointed to the figure on the right.

"That, my friend, is the figure of Justice."

Red Jacket withdrew his hand from his friend's arm and started to hasten away.

"Where him live now?" he asked.

This is the wit and not the language of which his friends have spoken, but it may be surmised that sometimes he deliberately feigned broken English to bring home a point.

One of the traits of the nonliterate Indians of the time was an accurate memory. In deep concentration, when addresses were made at Indian councils, the chiefs and even the women sought to memorize every statement and every circumstance. Every treaty was thus a living memory. The fact is well illustrated in a story of a hearing held by Governor Tompkins and the Seneca. An American agent while testifying made a statement that Red Jacket said was untrue.

"It is true," averred the agent. "It is on paper."

"The opposite is true. I have the facts written here," answered Red Jacket, pointing to his forehead.

"You have forgotten," retorted the agent, "the facts are written on paper."

"Then the paper lies."

With a patronizing smile the agent opened the docu-

ment, scanned it, and then with an apology said, "Well——
the chief is right."

Red Jacket's growing popularity put many lesser lights
in the shade, and his cutting arguments gave him success
so often that some of the more superstitious began to say
that only a sorcerer could have such power. Cornplanter
is said to have instigated this murmur, but it was Handsome Lake who made it effective for the good reason that
Red Jacket had lampooned him too often.

Thus the conspiracy against Red Jacket became an open
attack that was encouraged by the envious. Prompted by
Cornplanter's accusations and Handsome Lake's prophecies, a board of judges appointed by Cornplanter met,
heard the charges, and indicted the orator as a sorcerer.
The courts of the white men would not interfere, since
Red Jacket himself had proved that they had no jurisdic-
tion over internal Indian affairs. Under Indian law Red
Jacket, if found guilty, could be punished by death.

The leading Seneca of Buffalo and others from Allegany
and Cattaraugus were summoned; witnesses were primed
and ready with their perjuries; and all seemed to feel that
Red Jacket was now done for. Even the orator wondered
how he could extricate himself in the face of so many
enemies, but he resolved to make the boldest possible
defense, a defense in which he would show no mercy to
his accusers.

The tribal court gathered in a grove on the banks of
Buffalo Creek, and the judges listened to the charges.
They were cutting and venomous, all logic being sub-
merged in a morass of slander. The general feeling was that

facts weren't important because the victim was doomed in any event.

When his prosecutors had finished, Red Jacket arose, laid down his pipe, and walked to the center of the gathering. One against a nation, he stood, a target at which all could shoot. But were their arrows straight?

He looked each accuser in the face, nodding his head as if to say, "So that is the best you can do with lies!" Then he slowly began to analyze the character of his accusers, citing deed after deed that showed prejudice. His rapier thrusts went more deeply than any former utterance, and he brought forcefully to the attention of the crowd the numerous instances in which his enemies and accusers had been dishonest, weak, and utterly traitorous to the tribe. He branded every charge as false and defied the accusers to bring proof that was not perjured testimony. So convincingly did he do this that the mood of the crowd began to change. Far too many saw the deep truth the defendant was telling.

Wrapping his blanket about his athletic frame, he again looked each accuser in the eye, holding his gaze until heads were dropped and hands moved nervously. Then he gave a look of contempt and waved at the crowd with a smile and gesture that meant, "So that's that."

Then, with all the skill of a trained mind, he exposed the real reasons behind this disgraceful action of his tribesmen. He contrasted their lack of deeds with his own undoubted services, all of which his people had approved long before.

It was with relief that he noted the approving look on the faces of the people and saw them rise to shout, "You're right!" He again lashed out, saying, "Cornplanter, you're a cheat! You've heard me; and the Prophet is an impostor!" With that he returned to his seat.

The judges immediately retired but quickly came back to bring in the verdict, "Not guilty as charged!"

There were whoops and cheers at this evidently just and popular decision, but Red Jacket seemed unmoved. If he glanced at his accusers at all, it was a glance of supreme pity. Cornplanter was cut to the quick, and the Prophet slunk away, his face dark with fury. No reply ever was made to Red Jacket's countercharges, for he had proved them too well.

The white people who attended the trial soon spread the story, and interpreter Jones carefully kept in mind the circumstances of the ordeal. The news of the orator's undoubted victory even reached Governor De Witt Clinton, who remarked of it, "Perhaps the annals of history cannot furnish a more conspicuous triumph of the powers of oratory in a barbarous nation devoted to superstition. . . ."

After the trial Red Jacket went back to his cabin, but before long another conspiracy began to hatch. It was recalled that the orator had aspired to become one of the fifty sachems of the Six Nations, and it was remembered that he had risen only to the position of a subordinate called a pine-tree chief. His enemies, therefore, claimed that his ambition had been too great and urged that all title and all authority as a chief should be stripped from him as a punishment for lack of humility. He was branded an obstructionist, an agitator, an objector to progress. One of his own interpreters, the educated Dr. Jacob Jemison, drafted a complaint and charge demanding Red Jacket's expulsion from the council of chiefs.

"We renounce you as chief," the document read, "and from this time you are forbidden to act as such; all of our nation will hereafter regard you as a private man, and we say to them all, that everyone who shall do as you have done, if a chief, will in like manner be disowned by his brethren and set back where he started from."

The document was signed by twenty-one leading men, some of them progressive chiefs who had become members of the mission church. To his great sorrow the beleaguered old man saw the names of his former friends and comrades in arms, Young King, Captain Pollard, Little Billy, Seneca White, and others. Alas, he thought, even my old comrades have joined in the conspiracy against me! Like many another ambitious man who had gone too far, he had opposed popular movements and must suffer the penalty.

If he gave up now without a struggle, Red Jacket would be laid low in utter defeat. Greatly chagrined, he started for the national capital and succeeded in interviewing the Secretary of War and the chief of the Indian Bureau. He even tried to see the President.

The secretary told the tired man, whose chest still displayed the Washington medal, that he was well acquainted with the causes of the trouble and that the President also knew. The account shows that the secretary tried to convince Red Jacket that, if he had shown a spirit of tolerance and had allowed others the same freedom of religious thought that he claimed for himself, he would not have made enemies of the Christian Indians.

This wisdom strongly influenced Red Jacket and helped

him to adopt a new perspective. He abandoned his one-sided attitude and returned to Buffalo Creek determined to re-establish himself. Whatever one might believe about man's duty to his Creator, he now saw that, when there were differences in viewpoint, toleration must be expected and given. He swallowed his pride, called a council, and asked to have the charges reread. Chiefs had come from all the reservations to see that justice was done to one to whom they had every reason to be grateful, save for his ill-advised obstructionism.

Half Town, a Christian chief from Cattaraugus, began to speak for the defense. "There is but one voice from Cattaraugus," he said, "that of general indignation for the contumely cast upon a man as great as Red Jacket."

Other leading men were of the same opinion, and recited the many services which the deposed chief had rendered his people, often at the cost of long journeys and great exertion. They were not insensible of his human faults, they said, but likewise not ungrateful for his talents.

When no detractor now dared to raise his voice in opposition, the chiefs moved that the ouster be recalled and declared void. Red Jacket then was called to speak upon the subject, a right denied him when deposed.

"My brothers," he said sadly, "you have heard the statements of my associates in the council and their explanation of the foolish charges brought against me. I have taken the legal steps and the proper way to meet those charges. It is the only way I could notice them. They are charges I despise, which nothing could induce me to notice except the concern which many respected chiefs of my nation feel for the character of their aged comrade."

He looked about searchingly and went on. "Were it otherwise," he said, "I should not be before you now. I would fold my arms and sit quietly under these ridiculous slanders. The Christian party has not even proceeded legally, according to our usages, to put me down."

Red Jacket looked up with a gesture, sighed forgiveness for the mistake, and then spoke again.

"Ah, it grieves my heart when I look around me and see the situation of my people!" he exclaimed. "In old times they were united and powerful—now they are divided and feeble. When I am gone to the other world—when the Great Spirit calls me away—who among my people can take my place? Many years have I guided the nation."

There were tears in the old orator's eyes, and he could say no more. He took his seat and awaited the roll call on the motion to restore his rank.

The vote came and it was unanimous. He was a chief again!

But Red Jacket felt the lingering sting of the thorn even though it had been removed. Its pangs left him more mellow, more tolerant than before. Yet he was still unconvinced that his old formula was wrong. "First the missionary, then the rum seller, then the land-grabber and the loss of old homes, and then the whole story over once more." Nor was he wholly wrong in this; his error was in believing that the missionaries had been a cause of the land-grabbing by other whites.

Red Jacket's limited vision caused him to believe that a barrier against every circumstance that led to more encroachment must be built up and that this barrier must separate the minds as well as the properties of the two races. It was this that the western Indians were attempting to achieve, and the orator approved.

As the years came and went, Red Jacket had found his great ambition to be elected one of the ruling sachems of the Six Nations thwarted. Cornplanter and Handsome Lake had succeeded in preventing any consideration of his name as a candidate for the high office. He remained only a pine-tree chief, though his voice was stronger and his wisdom clearer than most others who had the honor of being one of the ruling fifty. More than this, with his fellow leaders he had seen the total eclipse of the power of the sachems and, indeed, their repudiation by the women at the Treaty of Big Tree as the price of security forever. Perhaps it was well that he was not a sachem now.

The trial of Red Jacket and his restoration had done much to bring about a new understanding, a greater tolerance, even of his enemies. His view of the character of the missionaries also had changed for the better, and a second mission in life dawned to Red Jacket.

Creed should not matter now; only the common welfare was important. He would declare this principle to all the people. Thus he called a council at which he declared the view he now entertained.

"It is not belief," he proclaimed, "but honestly serving the Creator and one's fellow men that counts. In seeking that greater good let us now be united."

[16] *WINTER SUNSET*

THOUGH RED JACKET long stood for the ancient ways of his people, he had gradually seen that the best interests of his nation lay in the acceptance of the material blessings of white civilization. He had seen that cattle supplied food and drink and that horses made travel easier. He had noted the usefulness of gristmills and sawmills and the advantage of the plow and other farming implements.

He realized that the implements of farming were those of peace and better living. He learned not to object to these things; but he was opposed to the acceptance of the beliefs and the attitudes of the white man. It was not the plow

that made the settler evil; it was what the white man desired the Indian to believe about the world and human
destiny. He didn't want missionaries and said so. He did
want the material advantages of the world of civilization
without accepting the institutions that had made these advantages possible. Thus his position often appeared inconsistent and confused. Indeed, he often reversed himself on vital questions or appeared to do so.

He distrusted the missionaries for their effort to instill
beliefs, but he trusted the Quakers because of their effort
to set an example and provide the tools of industry. The
Quakers were wise enough to sense that, if the Indians
were to accept white civilization, Quakers must demon-
strate its virtues by deed and honesty of purpose. By example they must show that what they had to offer was
better than what the Indian had. The red man's mind
would be prepared then for changes in his beliefs and
would make the change voluntarily. In this way nothing
would be imposed upon the Indian.

It was the supreme faith of the Quakers, "A tree is known
by its fruits," that spurred their endeavors with the New
York Indians. Since before the days of the Pickering treaty,
Red Jacket had trusted them, citing their generosity and
their lack of open hostility toward the native beliefs. The
Quakers reminded the Seneca people of this attitude in
an address that recalled Red Jacket's appeals to them for
advice and assistance.

"Brothers," they said, "you know very well that in extending you the hand of help we never had any private or
selfish views. We never wanted to take your lands nor your
timber nor anything that was yours. Nor did we intrude

ourselves among you or come to your assistance unasked or uninvited."

Then, referring to the appeals that had been made to them for protection, the Quaker spokesman proceeded to tell the Indians even more, reciting what Red Jacket had done in behalf of his people.

"Your late venerable chief, Red Jacket, foresaw that your reservations, though but a very small residue of your once widely extended territory, would in a few years become of great pecuniary value and greatly excite the avarice of the white man. Being an old man and feeling his health decline, he cast his eye around him to see where his people might find protection when he should be removed by death and the foot of their enemy might be placed upon his grave. Remembering the chain of friendship which had long bound his forefathers to the Society of Friends [Quakers] and the disinterested labors of that people for the benefit of the red man, he determined to apply for aid to the Committee on Indian Affairs. . . ."

In these words the Quakers explained Red Jacket's visit to New York City in 1827, stating that at that time he made a personal appeal, imploring aid because he believed that the very existence of the Seneca was in danger. Red Jacket had made this appeal following the forced sale of the Genesee Valley lands to the Ogden company. At that time, it will be recalled, Red Jacket had fought the sale. When a majority of his tribesmen had agreed to it, however, the chief had, according to custom, also signed the agreement to part with the land. He did this despite the fact that he had been told that he need not do so.

That there was nothing dishonest in his dealings is

shown by his continual warnings against the sale of more
land even though great pressure was brought through
rum, bribery, and threats or even the assurance that the
President of the United States wanted the sale to be made.
Red Jacket trusted few persons other than the stalwart
Quakers, who could not be intimidated and who were
quick to expose a fraud.

At the time of the appeal of 1827, the Quakers were
expending their resources to help the Onondaga nation and
did not see the way clear to respond immediately to the
needs of the Seneca. Of this incident the Quakers wrote,
"On hearing the decision the old chief was very sorrowful
and appeared greatly dejected. He returned to his nation
with the sad tidings, but although he was cast down, he
was not in despair."

Two years later Red Jacket again appealed to the Friends
to take his people under their care. "I am now very old," he
told them with much feeling, "and must soon be gathered
to the tomb of my fathers. If now I could only have the
assurance that after my decease my nation would have the
protection of Friends, my path to the grave would be made
smooth and I could die in peace." It was his last request,
and thereafter the Society of Friends made an all-out en-
deavor to assist the Seneca people both with farm implements and with sound advice. Within ten years they were
to engage in a campaign to expose as a heartless fraud the
renewed dealings of the Ogden Land Company. This was
the undercover efforts of the land company to get possession of every acre owned by Indians in New York State. By
1838 it succeeded in doing this in a transaction so villainous
that the courts voided the transaction.

Red Jacket had cautioned his people of this new disaster, but his warnings proved unavailing. Yet the Society
of Friends remained vigilant and faithful. Their documents
exposing the transactions constitute an almost unknown
history of "the revolting fact that, in order to drive these
poor Indians from their lands, deception and fraud had
been practiced to an extent, perhaps without parallel in
the dark history of oppression and wrong, to which the
aborigines of our country have been subjected." But Red
Jacket did not live to know the aftermath of his warnings,
and his detractors could not now accuse him of having en-
gineered the fraud and having profited by it.

The last years of the old chief's life were years of effort to
save his people from the doom that he foresaw and sought
to avert. The intemperance of which some accused him
was, if it existed, in all probability the reflection of his fears
rather than addiction to alcohol. Indeed, his white friends
of Buffalo deny that he was the habitual drunkard that
some have accused him of being. It is to be noted that
the Quakers who dealt with him did not mention this as a
characteristic of the chief.

Busy with journeys to New York and Philadelphia during his last decade of life, Red Jacket called upon his faithful friends, imploring them to see that justice was done
the Seneca people. He was often serious but quite as often
enjoyed a visit for the sake of comradeship. There was a
certain nostalgic restlessness as he passed his seventieth
year, a new eagerness to live again the pleasures of his
youth. Yet no opportunity was lost to appeal to the conscience of his white neighbors or to implore his own race

to firmly stand for their best interests and not to sell more land. It was his constant theme.

Throughout his life the orator enjoyed wandering amid his old haunts and among old friends. He had long trusted Horatio Jones, the white captive who had become an army captain and interpreter for the Indians. In some way, however, a suspicion had been planted that Jones had aided the land companies in deceiving the Seneca and that he was actually an enemy. Thus, though Jones bore an Indian name and had lived with the Seneca for many years, receiving from them large land grants, Red Jacket had a deep suspicion that he might be a traitor.

On one journey across the Genesee, Red Jacket stopped at the Timothy Hosmer Inn at Avon, and there he saw Jones but did not greet him. Jones, however, had no sense of guilt and advanced with his usual cordiality, extending his hand. Red Jacket looked at his erstwhile friend with disdain, uttering a word of scorn.

"What troubles you?" asked Jones.

"And you at last have deserted us," replied Red Jacket. It is said that Jones wept like a child and emphatically denied that he had ever been disloyal to the Seneca. When he was convinced that his friend was still faithful, Red Jacket, forgetful of the stoicism of his race, also wept. He and his friend embraced with old-time heartiness. Faith was restored and never clouded again.

Invited to the Jones home for dinner, the old Seneca chief was welcomed by Mrs. Jones who was quite fond of him, for he was always a gracious guest.

Mrs. Jones later told of the incident and confessed that

she had played a joke on him. She knew how fond of sugar Red Jacket was, but when she laid his coffee before him, she purposely neglected to offer him the sugar bowl, wishing to see if he would ask for it.

Her guest, however, never liked to be trifled with, for somehow any playful attempt to ruffle his dignity hurt his pride. Upon noticing the furtive glances of the family, he realized that something was afoot and began to stir his coffee with great vigor as if trying to discover the needed ingredient.

"My son," he exclaimed, speaking to Mr. Jones, "do you allow your wife to thus trifle with your father?"

Then noting that the children were giggling as if they had knowledge of the joke, he spoke again.

"And, my son, do you allow your children to make sport of their chief?"

His distress was so apparent that both Captain and Mrs. Jones apologized and, to make amends, passed the sugar bowl with a flourish.

Red Jacket looked at the sugar, turned the bowl upside down, and poured the sweetening into his cup, filling it to the brim. Then without batting an eye, he began with great gusto to eat it with his spoon, exclaiming, "*Oguhoh!*", "It is good!"

The children were now popeyed, and their parents were purple with suppressed amusement. Yet they might have known that Red Jacket never missed some response to a challenge. He loved to turn the tables.

At this particular time Red Jacket had brought along his gun, hoping to hunt north of Jones' Bridge. With his stepson Dan Two Guns, he crossed the river and pressed northward toward his old hunting lodge on Fall Brook. He found no sign of it, and so, hefting his gun, he pushed through the woods still to the north, looking for old and familiar oaks. No game appeared anywhere, and soon they came out in a clearing. Still walking on, the hunters came to another forest growth, but this, too, was not a hiding place for deer. In a moment the hunters plunged against a fence and looked out at a plowed field. Red Jacket stopped short and grounded his gun. Was this the old region where once he had roamed carefree? Was this the land upon which Morris had said that the Seneca might hunt forever?

He leaped the fence and looked out over the land; at the far end of the field he saw a farmer plowing. With this he shut his eyes and slumped down in an angle of the fence, his whole body quivering.

The poet Bryant, in "An Indian at the Burial Place of His Fathers," pictures in one stanza what was in the mind of Red Jacket when he found his hunting grounds destroyed.

> Methinks it were a nobler sight
> To see these vales in woods arrayed,
> Their summits in the golden light,
> Their trunks in grateful shade,
> And herds of deer, that bounding go,
> O'er rills and prostrate trees below.

The waning health of Red Jacket made his friends wonder how long he would survive the continued shocks that came to him.

Nor was Red Jacket destined to live for many months more. He sensed his approaching hour and urged his reservation friends to remain faithful to the best interests of their people. For the last time he summoned a council at which he expanded upon the once happy condition of the Seneca when they were free to roam over a wide territory that was all their own. Now the lakes and the streams, the deep ravines, and the waterfalls were in other hands, and with them were the old clearings where villages had once stood and where the graves of their fathers were hidden. Now towns of the rising American nation covered the land, and old and favorite forests had been hewn down. New diseases had come and carried away hundreds of their people—yes, thousands—within his memory. Something called "money" was now a goal; something called "civilization" was a new way of life.

Always an idealist who saw only the unalloyed goodness of the old way, he pictured the glory of the past against the decadence of the present, quite forgetting that even in the old days there were cruelties and injustice. All this was forgotten, even the question of his stepson who had asked if the Indian should always remain like an acorn and not grow from a germ to a mighty oak. "Why always be an acorn or mourn because it has fallen to pieces as it sent up a sapling?" Two Guns had asked.

He did not think of this now, but he did go on to say to his council, "Unite, my brethren! Only by holding together in one great purpose, that of holding your lands, can we defeat the desire of land-grabbers to take all we have. Never mind the differences in religious belief. We are free to believe what we wish, and let the Great Spirit decide in his own time what is right. Let our children go to the mission school if it does them good; they may find new light if they climb high. Let us have schools as planned, and let our parents decide whether their children shall attend here or at Tunesassa where the good Quakers teach. I now offer this resolution, that we give the hand of freedom to all and tell the missionaries of our gratitude and kindly feeling. The past is gone—let us look forward now."

In this way Red Jacket, without directly expressing any change in his religious beliefs, extended freedom of thought and freedom of worship to those who differed with him. But there is every reason to think that Mrs. Jacket, whose exemplary life was an occasion of remark, had influenced the heart of Red Jacket.

"When I am gone," he said with sadness in his voice as he drew his halting speech to a close, "when I am gone, my warning shall no longer be heard, and the craft and avarice of the white man will prevail. Many winters have I breasted the storm. I am an aged tree and can stand no longer. My leaves have fallen, my branches are withered, and I am shaken with every breeze. Soon my aged trunk will be prostrate, and the foot of the exulting foe may be placed upon it in safety. I will have none who will be able to avenge such an indignity.

"Think not, my people, that I mourn for myself. I go to join the spirits of my fathers, where age cannot wither; but my heart fails when I think of my people, who are soon to be scattered and forgotten."

After this, his last speech in a council, Red Jacket went from house to house, trying to make his comrades see that, whether Christians or not, all Indians should be united in the bonds of their racial ties.

Mrs. Jacket, when she heard of her husband's stand in the interests of a new religious freedom, moved to a new cabin quite near the mission church and school, and Red Jacket dutifully followed. It was easier to attend the church services now, and the children enjoyed the convenience of having their friends nearer.

Exhausted by his last efforts, during the early days of January, 1830, Red Jacket took to his bed, lying long hours in silence. He was weak and evidently in pain. Yet he was patient and made few demands.

"Mother, Mother," he said faintly one morning, "I have said strong words against Mr. Harris; I have accused him of things he never has done. I am not angry at him; I have only been afraid that, if we obeyed his words, we should become like white people. I see now that this is not so; Christian Indians are still Indians. Have Mr. Harris come; I want to talk with him."

The old chief fell into silence again, but his eyes were bright. Suddenly he spoke again. "Mother," he said, "find my vial of water. I have always treasured that water; it came from the spring where I was born. Many times I have gone there when I was on a journey, and I drank of the spring where my mother dipped when I was young."

Mrs. Jacket hunted through the trinket bags and treasure baskets brought from the old cabin and finally found the vial of water in a medicine bag.

"Good," he said, "now place it in my hand. When I die, I will have this wonderful water to take with me."

"You must not die," answered Mrs. Jacket. "I will get a doctor in Buffalo. He will give you the white man's medicine. You look very ill."

"No white doctor can cure me now," said Red Jacket. "This water in my hand is all I need."

He called his stepchildren to him and sent for the Two Guns boys, Daniel and Henry, both Christians now. Harris could not be reached.

Little Ruth bathed his fevered forehead with water and heard his thanks.

"If I could have lived," said the dying man to his wife, "I should have built you a new house. I am sorry I ever left you because of your new faith; I treated you unkindly."

Pressing little Ruth's hand, he spoke to her, and she remembered his words as long as she lived. They were words of advice on how to guard her own girlhood years and find happiness in her maturity. Then he turned his head, looking up at Mrs. Jacket.

"Where is the missionary?" he asked. "Tell him that I do not hate him."

He closed his eyes, becoming delirious. He murmured that his old comrades were around him, some chiding him for his mistakes and urging him to see that there was a task ahead. He thought Farmer's Brother was there and wondered why he had come. "Why should he trouble me now?" he asked.

Ruth was still holding his hand when he shuddered, grasped her, and held her to his chest—and then expired.

There was no death wail at the door, only the stifled sobs of his wife and the tread of the feet of those who were busy with the task of caring for his body. This was done by the Two Guns boys and by interpreter Jones who had been asked to arrange the funeral.

Though Red Jacket had held aloof from the white man's

religion, it was in a home of Christian men and women
that he had passed away on January 20, 1830. It was the
eve of the Indian new year, when the Great Spirit was
thanked in detail for all the blessings mankind had received and the new year was greeted by a nine-day festival of song and ceremony. Yet these rites were now
merged in the new religion of Handsome Lake, and this
was not Red Jacket's religion.

According to his request he was buried with a simple
service that was neither Christian nor pagan, in a Christian cemetery, by Christian men and women, and among
the great chiefs who had died in the new faith.

What had he meant when he said, "I do not hate the
missionary"?

Perhaps it was again to say, "We do not want to take
your religion from you; we only want to enjoy our own."

More than likely, however, it meant that he wanted to
thank Harris for the good he had done and to say that no
longer did he mistrust the motives of men and women
who had brought about so great a change in the lives of
his people.

Long after the orator had gone to his rest, his bones
were taken up to preserve them from the rapidly growing
city that by 1850 had spread out to absorb the old Buffalo Creek reservation. When Ruth Two Guns Stevenson
heard of the violation of the grave, she sent her brother
to reclaim the crumbling remains. Recovered, they were
taken to the Cattaraugus reservation, where they were
kept in a small casket until 1884 when, amid city-wide
ceremony, they were reburied in the shadow of an impressive monument. Most of the other chiefs of Red

Jacket's time were then removed from the burial ground and reinterred in a circle around the monument.

The memorial, later topped by a bronze statue paid for by Mrs. Jacob Huyler, stands in Forest Lawn, Buffalo, New York. Its initial cost was defrayed by a committee of citizens, and the exercises were arranged by the officers of the Buffalo Historical Society. As was fitting, there were many Six Nations Indians present. Among them were several who had seen Red Jacket in their younger days. Ruth Stevenson was there to weep silently again but to rejoice that her stepfather at last was in a fitting resting place.

One may wonder why an old Indian who could neither read nor write had earned this respect from those whose ancestors he had opposed. Even the children of the Buffalo schools were asking that question, for somehow Red Jacket had become a leading name with which the growing city was associated. There were Red Jacket clubs, Red Jacket athletic teams, Red Jacket brands of food—and two biographies of note.

Somehow Red Jacket had done something to make himself Buffalo's most eminent character, its most outstanding personality. What was it, then, that his successors saw implicit in his life?

The answer is this: Red Jacket more than any other man of his time challenged the sincerity of our civilization, and by his criticism he lifted a mirror to its face—though few at the time opened their eyes to see the distorted picture. He pointed out the weakness of our approach in missionary effort, and he unmasked the hidden forces that served to undermine and destroy the objectives of law and religion. He saw too far ahead and he was too far in advance, that was all. Like all leaders in thought, he found himself looked upon with awe but as a thing apart. His own people repudiated him twice, and many tried to smear his name. Only a few white citizens of his generation understood him, though many more admired him. Not so, however, with the keen sons of progress who wanted the land of his fathers. To them he was the personification of obstruction, a barrier to progress—their progress.

Fifty-four years after his death, Red Jacket was a chief topic of conversation in Buffalo, and the community that had blotted out the little Indian villages sought to accord him a deserved recognition. Leading citizens now had found a local hero. Historians, poets, students of racial patterns, all began to see a deep significance in his thinking and a clue to the process of culture rivalries. It was then that Buffalo sought to honor its unique personality and reappraise his character.

The callousness of his own generation, however, is typical of the disregard of all prophets. His own people had been deaf to his warnings against the land buyers and had eagerly swallowed the bait that had trapped them. Though he had amply justified his council name, He keeps them awake, his people had been awake with closed eyes. When, in the end, they did open their eyes and rub them, they beheld a transformed world that was not of their own making. No longer could they be Indians; for sheer survival they were compelled to make an adjustment. Nor had his white neighbors fully understood him or realized what he had meant when he counseled them to live in accordance with the morals their religious men preached. To those who had been concerned with getting land and profiting by it, ideals were not regarded as practical guides—for them.

Thousands of settlers had come into western New York following the Treaty of Big Tree and the Ogden purchase. Red Jacket during the last years of his life was never far from new clearings in the woodland or from great piles of uprooted trees and burning brush. The plow tore through the ashes of old Indian villages and disturbed crumbling bones. The streams where once he fished for trout and pickerel were choked with sawdust or harnessed to mills. In all this Red Jacket saw the rising force of the white man's progress. It was a restless effort to find a more comfortable living, a better supply of food, a world in which youth might have a better chance. That this effort would benefit his own race, he did not foresee; nor did he live to witness the transformation of his people. He could only mourn as he saw towns rise where only a forest had been, churches lift their spires to the sky, and schoolhouses rise in sheltered valleys. The sounds of the hammer and saw, the ringing of bells, and the clang of the anvil were not music to him. They were threats and not promises of good to come.

Perhaps few of his generation could have described the crumbling of Red Jacket's world as did the son of his one-time interpreter, William H. C. Hosmer, who had often visited the chief when he came to Canawaugus, opposite Avon on the Genesee. Of the changes that had come Hosmer wrote:

Realm of the Seneca, no more
In shadow lies the Pleasant Vale;
Gone are the chiefs who ruled of yore,
Like chaff before the rushing gale.

Their rivers run with narrowed bounds,
Cleared are their broad, old hunting grounds,
And on their ancient battlefields
The greensward to the plowman yields.

Like mocking echoes of the hill
Their fame resounded and grew still;
And on green ridge and level plain
Their hearths will never smoke again.

NOTE ON RED JACKET'S PORTRAITS

As RED JACKET's fame grew, poets wrote verses about him and artists often asked him to pose. It is quite likely that sketches were made of him, but until his later years he shied away from invitations to sit for his portrait. "I do not want a picture of me to outlast me," he once said.

The reluctance to have his likeness painted may have been due to the superstition, such as was held by some Indians in those days, that a picture captures the soul of a man and makes him a captive; or it may have been a form of false pride.

The time came, however, when Red Jacket changed his mind about sitting for his portrait. In his travels he had often seen the pictures of prominent men hung in public places and in stately homes. It was this fact perhaps that finally caused him to give his consent when J. L. D. Mathies, a Canandaigua artist, asked him to make three sittings. Posing for Mathies provided the chief his first experiences with keeping quiet and appearing to be unconcerned while someone studied him intently. Nevertheless, he was greatly interested in the picture as it began to appear on the canvas, and he carefully watched it as it progressed.

Red Jacket was morose at the time, fearing, as he did, that the land companies would succeed in their attempt to take away the Seneca lands at Buffalo. The portrait undoubtedly shows the strain caused by his concern for the future of his people. Some who have examined the painting have said that the face reveals cynicism and the dissipation of which Red Jacket was often accused. An editorial in a Canandaigua paper, however, commented on the excellence of the painting, in the flowery manner of that day, as follows:

His bold and high arch'd forehead, his deeply indented brow, where thought seems to have worn channels that testify its strength; his face fierce and determined glance, and the peculiar conformation of his lips where eloquence has spent its most commanding tones; these, and in truth all the prominent features of the chief, are now upon canvas. . . .

Orsamus Turner, who wrote the *History of the Holland Purchase*, saw the painting before 1855 and said, "It is the portrait of Red Jacket as he was, and as he looked; the

Red Jacket of the Seneca reservation . . . as lifelike upon canvas as the poet made him on the lettered page."

Turner should have known, for he said, "We have seen him in his wigwam; in the council house of his nation, swaying the minds of his people more by his masterly eloquence than by means of any special love they entertained for him; upon the war and peace path; in his moods of subtle stoicism; in his gayer hours; in his hunter's camp; in a log cabin carousal." And Turner liked the picture, perhaps because it recalled the incidents and places to which he referred. But whether it truly was a likeness of the man, we cannot be sure.

In 1827, as we have said, Red Jacket and a Seneca delegation visited New York City to ask the Quakers to assist his people with their agricultural and social problems and to look into the encroachments of settlers. The elite of the city welcomed the famous orator, and he made a number of new acquaintances. Among them was a New York physician, Dr. J. W. Francis, who was attracted to Red Jacket.

The doctor approached R. W. Weir, one of the noted artists of the city, and asked him to paint the chief's picture if a sitting could be arranged. The artist was agreeable, and Red Jacket, when invited to pose, consented.

To put the chief at ease, the artist and physician talked about diseases among Indians and the cures that were recommended. Since Red Jacket prided himself upon his knowledge of herbs and considered himself quite a doctor, this was a subject that occupied his mind while the artist worked.

When sitting for Weir, the chief was dressed in the

costume he thought appropriate. He wore a caped coat with braid and tassels, girded himself with a red sash, arranged his Washington medal, grasped his pipe tomahawk, and stood with it resting upon a support that is shown in the picture as a rock. His Indian comrades sat on the floor, smoking as they watched the picture grow.

Working for two or three hours a day for four or five days, the artist plied his brushes and finished his task. At intervals during this time the orator was allowed to relax and converse. He was interested in the completion of each detail of his dress and was pleased that the artist had granted his wish that Niagara Falls appear in the background of the painting. He expressed satisfaction, too, when the artist had put the finishing touches on the Washington medal.

Other portraits and drawings of Red Jacket, sometimes slightly modified, have been reproduced in books describing Indian life. An excellent painting by R. M. Sully is owned by the Pennsylvania Historical Society. Time and the shrinking of the paint, however, have marred it somewhat. From it was probably made the lithograph by an unknown artist which is now owned by the Redwood (New York) Library. There are a score of paintings and lithographs in the archives of several local societies, but it is doubtful that Red Jacket posed for them.

The recorded impressions of those who were well acquainted with Red Jacket give valuable information concerning his appearance and character. John James Audubon, Thomas Morris, Orsamus Turner, and Lafayette are among those who have commented upon his appearance or who have described his conversation. Some caught the humor, the dry wit, of the man who on occasion represented himself as ignorant of the conventions of society in order to create the text of a humorous episode.

This is illustrated by a conversation with General Lafayette. The two met like old friends, each looking at the other with interest.

"Ah, General," exclaimed Red Jacket, speaking through his interpreter, "time has not been so severe upon you as it has with me. It has left you a fresh countenance and hair to cover your head; while me——behold!"

Lifting a handkerchief from his head with an air of much feeling, he revealed that he was nearly bald. Those who heard this retort could not help laughing at the simplicity of the Indian (who, after all, was angling for his joke).

The general then gracefully disclosed the fact that his hair was only a wig. But Red Jacket, pretending to mistake the wig for a scalp, is said to have exclaimed, "Ugh! I never conceived the idea of regarnishing my head at the expense of one of my neighbors."

General Lafayette's secretary, who was present at the time, later described Red Jacket's appearance. "This extraordinary man, although much worn down by time and intemperance," he wrote, "preserves yet, in a surprising degree, the exercise of all his faculties. He obstinately refuses to speak any language but that of his own people and affects a great dislike to all others, although it is easy to discern that he perfectly understands English."

Thomas Morris, whom Red Jacket distrusted after the Treaty of Big Tree, was another who has left us a description of the old chief. "His stature was rather above than below middle size," Morris wrote. "He was well-made. His eyes were fine and expressive of the intellect of which he possessed an uncommon portion. His address, particularly when he spoke in council, was very fine and almost majestic."

A year after the chief's portrait had been painted in New York, the celebrated artist George Catlin came to Buffalo seeking the privilege of painting his portrait. Red Jacket felt that Catlin was a sincere and capable man. Moreover, he had lost any reluctance for having his likeness reproduced, and the possibility that it might be hung with portraits of other notables in public places pleased him. He liked the background of the Weir portrait and told Catlin that again he wanted Niagara Falls in the picture. This time, however, the painting of the falls must be done at the actual site and not from imagination.

Of the portrait, Catlin wrote, "So I painted his portrait from life in the costume in which he is represented [in the painting] and indulged him also in the wish he had expressed, that he might be seen standing on Table Rock at the Falls of Niagara about which he thought his spirit would linger after he was dead. . . ." Commenting upon the subject uppermost in Red Jacket's mind, Catlin said, "Poor old chief—not all the eloquence of Cicero or Demosthenes would be able to avert the calamity that awaits his declining nation—to resist the despoiling hand of mercenary white men that opens and spreads liberally only to entrap the unwary and ignorant within its grasp."

The Catlin painting shows the old chief—he was seventy-seven years old then—as he wanted to be remembered rather than as the artist might have wished to pose him, for it is not an artist's pose. It shows Red Jacket wearing a Seneca hat with two drooping eagle plumes and leggings and moccasins that were correct Seneca apparel. Of interest are his powerful arms, the right hanging down and the left with extended forefinger pointing at the falls. It was this feature of the background that he insisted upon, for he often said that his spirit would linger there after death. Within a year after he had spoken of this to Catlin, his spirit did pass from its earthly form. If ever a ghost is seen in the spray of Niagara on moonlight nights, it will be that of the historic Red Jacket more appropriately than that of the mythical "maid of the mist."

INDEX